JANE AUSTEN AND THE DIDACTIC NOVEL

JANE AUSTEN AND THE DIDACTIC NOVEL

Northanger Abbey, Sense and Sensibility and *Pride and Prejudice*

Jan Fergus

BARNES & NOBLE BOOKS
TOTOWA, NEW JERSEY

First published in the USA 1983 by
BARNES & NOBLE BOOKS
81 Adams Drive, Totowa,
New Jersey, 07512

ISBN 0-389-20228-2

Printed in Hong Kong

Library of Congress Cataloging in Publication Data

Fergus, Jan S., 1943–
Jane Austen and the didactic novel

Bibliography: p.
Includes index.
1. Austen, Jane, 1775-1817—Criticism and interpreta-
tion. I. Title.
PR4037.F47 1983   823'.7   81-12773
ISBN 0-389-20228-2   AACR2

In memory of
Charlotte Johnson Fergus
John Edward Fergus

Contents

Acknowledgments

It is a great pleasure to thank those whose help enabled me to complete this book. Irving Howe and Frank Brady of the Graduate School, City University of New York, have been extremely generous with advice, criticism and encouragement. And without much more of the same at many stages from my friends, especially Ginger Hjelmaa, Viiu Menning and Ruth Portner, the book would never have been finished.

All citations of Jane Austen's fiction are based on the editions of R. W. Chapman, 5 vols, 3rd edn (Oxford, 1933) and *Minor Works*, vol. VI (Oxford, 1954) by permission of Oxford University Press. Page references are inserted directly into the text. Where any ambiguity may occur, the following abbreviations apply:

NA	*Northanger Abbey*
SS	*Sense and Sensibility*
PP	*Pride and Prejudice*
MP	*Mansfield Park*
E	*Emma*
P	*Persuasion*
MW	*Minor Works*

Page references to the following editions are also inserted directly into the text, using these abbreviations:

L   *Jane Austen's Letters to her Sister Cassandra and Others*, ed. R. W. Chapman, 2nd edn 1952, rpt 1964 (London: Oxford University Press).

SL   *Selected Letters of Samuel Richardson*, ed. and intro. John Carroll (Oxford: Clarendon Press, 1964). (Indications of Richardson's verbal changes, noted by Carroll, are omitted.)

Introduction

In Jane Austen's early novels, *Northanger Abbey, Sense and Sensibility* and *Pride and Prejudice,* a great artist can be observed in the process of extending her range and mastering her craft. Each of these novels draws upon and betters the achievement of the previous one in an artistic development that is highly complex yet remarkably continuous and coherent, lacking the uncertainties which usually accompany experiment and growth. All three novels succeed in their aims, if rightly understood, and these aims are relatively accessible, for the early novels display their themes openly and clearly. This openness separates them from the later novels, *Mansfield Park, Emma* and *Persuasion,* whose greater density can sometimes obscure or complicate their aims and methods. The early novels are also 'literary', very explicitly borrowing from, measuring themselves against or transforming eighteenth-century models, and therefore inviting and rewarding comparison with these models. The later novels largely abandon literary jokes and referents, and to compare them with eighteenth-century novels does little to yield a clearer view of their techniques and concerns. What can illuminate the last three novels, however, is comparison with each other and with the first three. The early novels have, then, a special significance for students of Austen and particularly for attempts to define her achievement. Nonetheless, Virginia Woolf's well-known judgment that 'of all great writers she is the most difficult to catch in the act of greatness'[1] holds for any critical approach.

To speak of Jane Austen's technique of allusiveness or her development as an artist is certainly not new. These are endlessly discussed by twentieth-century critics.[2] Nineteenth-century critics succeeded in articulating the possible views of Austen's intentions: for them, she is variously a realist, humorist, didact, ironist, moralist and social critic. These categories either overlap or partially contradict each other. The social critic may be at odds with the realist: contemporaries of Austen who praised her faithful portraits of everyday social life apparently did not notice her astringent criticisms of the society she portrays. The contradiction is resolved, usually, by pointing to Austen's irony, which permits her to remain uncommitted or to have it both ways, to 'cherish and abominate' the world she lives in, which is also the world she describes in

1

her novels.[3] But this resolution entails further difficulties. If Austen intends to be an ironist, as detached and uncommitted as some critics assert, other critics ask how she can be a moralist as well, committed to exploring the relations of reason and feeling, or manners and morals, in order to affirm those values all readers detect in her work: good principle, good judgment and good feeling. Similarly, if she is a humorist and an entertainer, delighting in folly and absurdity, how can she be didactic, intending to instruct and improve her readers?

These contradictions may be more apparent than real. Austen's moral seriousness and her characteristic irony have been easily reconciled by those critics prepared to accept an ironic attitude as valuable in itself. Accordingly, an excessive and even dogmatic appreciation of irony is detectable in studies of Austen through the 1940s and early 1950s.[4] Subsequent criticism has found this attitude unhistorical, and corrects it by emphasizing the positive moral values in Austen's work as these are revealed through her language or through her debts to the ideas and fiction of her contemporaries. Most of the volumes of criticism published during the last twenty years adopt one or both of these approaches, for they cannot be wholly separated. Even so, linguistic and historical criticism differ from each other in approaching Austen's meaning. Linguistic studies emphasize the expressiveness of her style. Her vocabulary is capable of registering the finest discriminations among moral and social values, while her narrative techniques allow full expression to the emotions and thoughts of her characters. For linguistic critics, Austen's language articulates and confirms her moral seriousness. Historical studies point out precedents for Austen's themes and treatment in eighteenth-century thought and fiction and, more recently, note parallels between her concerns and those of the Romantic movement.[5]

Mary Lascelles' *Jane Austen and her Art*, which remains the finest single work on Austen, contains the first sustained treatment of the relations between Austen and her predecessors in the novel. Subsequent critics have extended her study. Nevertheless, most critics after Lascelles fail to discover relationships between Austen's novels and her predecessors' which are interesting or significant enough to clarify Austen's achievements, probably because few modern critics can share Austen's delight in eighteenth-century popular fiction. The distance between the frequent crudeness of form, style and substance in the second-rate novels Austen is known to have read (and even admired) and the mastery displayed in her own fiction is so immense that critics hardly know what to make of any parallels they do find. As a rule, either they consider the parallels sufficiently interesting in themselves or they ignore them, taking refuge in wonder at Austen's ability to transcend such limitations.

Linguistic and historical approaches to Austen share one great advantage: they do not encourage assertions of her limitations. Instead, they register even more fully than earlier criticism the depth of her moral seriousness. Formerly, to assert Austen's limitations had been so conventional among her critics that in 1963, Ian Watt could write that 'the enduring problem of Jane Austen criticism' is the problem of 'scale versus stature; the slightness of the matter and the authority of the manner'.[6] Recent critics reject this view of the 'matter' as slight, most convincingly by reaffirming that the world Austen describes is the one we live in, and that she makes this world 'luminous' with meaning.[7]

My own view is similar: Austen's limits are those of ordinary life and thus render her work immediate, compelling, powerful, and significant to a degree unequalled elsewhere. Like the historical critics, I approach the literary techniques which shape Austen's early novels, and the artistic development visible in them, through eighteenth-century models which influence or are reflected in *Northanger Abbey, Sense and Sensibility,* and *Pride and Prejudice.* I differ from many modern critics in considering Austen's intentions primarily didactic. Nineteenth-century critics do speak of Austen as a didactic novelist, but in passing. The best of them rather assume than explicate Austen's intentions to instruct her readers.[8] Some modern critics also suggest that Austen intends to educate her audience. Among them is David Lodge, who asserts, in his fine study of the vocabulary in *Mansfield Park,* that 'she puts every generation of readers to school, and in learning her own subtle and exact vocabulary of discrimination and evaluation, we submit to the authority of her vision, and recognize its relevance to our own world of secularized spirituality'.[9] Austen's readers learn more, however, than a 'vocabulary of discrimination' from *Mansfield Park* or the other novels. Austen educates her readers' judgments and sympathies.[10] She intends to instruct and to refine the emotions along with the perceptions and the moral sense. This intention was shared by many of her predecessors in the novel, but none of them anticipates her success, partly because they lack her genius, but also because received ideas about literature, its function, and especially its effect on readers did not encourage the development in the novel of literary conventions which could genuinely delight and instruct.[11]

J. M. S. Tompkins' excellent study of the popular novel in the late eighteenth century documents these received ideas about the functions of literature, ideas which were applied with special zeal to novels, and she concludes: 'The champions of the novel . . . took up for the most part the old *utile dulci* line of defence that had served Sidney to vindicate "delightful feigning". Either the novel teaches directly, by way of moral doctrine and general information, or it educates the emotions and, by displaying various types of human nature, acquaints the reader vicariously with the world.'[12] Of these alternatives, the first is less interesting to Austen. Her characters sometimes debate moral doctrine, and precepts of various kinds can be extracted from her works, but a glance at almost any eighteenth-century novel, even *Clarissa* and *Tom Jones*, will reveal how comparatively little concern Austen has to teach directly in this manner. She is far more interested in an attempt to 'educate the emotions', and so were Richardson and Fielding, however willing they may have been also to teach 'directly, by way of moral doctrine and general information'.

Emotional didacticism, in this sense, is no simple task, and was made no easier by eighteenth-century notions of the effects of literature on readers' emotions and judgments. According to moralists of the period, readers were likely to imitate the actions and adopt the sentiments of characters in fiction, much as modern audiences are supposed by modern moralists to be inclined to violence because they are so exposed to it in films, television and newspapers. Samuel Johnson formulates the moral problem which results for novelists when life is assumed to imitate art in this way, and dictates the eighteenth-century solution of the problem in *Rambler* No. 4: 'But if the power of example is so great, as to take possession of the memory by a kind of violence, and produce effects almost without the intervention of the will, care ought to be taken that, when the choice is unrestrained, the best examples only should be exhibited; and that which is likely to operate so strongly, should not be mischievous or uncertain in its effects.'[13] The logical but unfortunate consequence of this position, if Johnson's qualifying 'when the choice is unrestrained'[14] is disregarded, will be a character like Richardson's perfect hero, Sir Charles Grandison. But if Richardson's choice is better exercised, that is, when his moral purpose requires an exemplary but imperfect heroine and an attractive villain, then his emotional didacticism can be successful. Its success was acknowledged by Johnson himself when he wrote that in *Clarissa*, Richardson 'enlarged the knowledge of human nature, and taught the passions to move at the command of virtue'.[15] Nonetheless, exemplary characters were thought safest. For if the 'main business' of the eighteenth-century novel was 'to inculcate morality by example',[16] then a perfect example must be the most efficacious, or at least the most innocuous: 'no harm can possibly arise from the imitation of a perfect character, though the attempt should fall short of the original'.[17]

These notions certainly did not prevent eighteenth-century novelists from attempting what was known as the 'mixed character', but they may have interfered with the eighteenth-century reader's ability to interpret or respond to such characters correctly. The unwarranted admiration and sympathy that Richardson's readers felt for Lovelace are as notorious and well-documented as are the consequences: Richardson's exasperation, his explanatory footnotes to *Clarissa,* and his 'good man', Sir Charles Grandison. Yet Richardson declared himself unwilling to read *Tom Jones* partly because he was so shocked at what he had heard of the hero's mixed character. He concluded that Fielding wrote the novel with a 'View . . . to whiten a vicious Character, and to make Morality bend to his Practices' (*SL,* p. 127).[18] Fanny Burney's diary records instances of her readers' inability to appreciate her mixed character, Mrs Delvile, in *Cecilia.* Her readers wanted a character to be all good or all bad, were baffled when Mrs Delvile was not, and accused Burney of making her inconsistent.[19]

The common reader's recalcitrance does not seem to trouble Austen. However comfortable the eighteenth-century reader may have been with the perfect characters who became a convention of didacticism, Austen refuses to cater to this taste, or, rather, she sees its dangers. Although she accepts the eighteenth-century doctrine that literature should educate the emotions and the judgment, she rejects most of the literary conventions associated with the doctrine, and particularly the exemplary character. Her criticism of this convention is implicit in her choice of imperfect heroes or heroines for her novels and explicit in a letter to her niece, Fanny Knight, who has relayed the criticism of a reader (one closely resembling those Burney describes in her diary). Austen's reply is playful, but penetrating: 'Do not oblige him to read any more. . . . He & I should not in the least agree of course, in our ideas of Novels and Heroines; – pictures of perfection as you know make me sick & wicked – but there is some very good sense in what he says, & I particularly respect him for wishing to think well of all young Ladies; it shews an amiable & a delicate Mind. – And he deserves better treatment than to be obliged to read any more of my Works' (*L,* pp. 486–7).

Austen rejects perfect heroines because they create emotional and moral responses precisely the reverse of edifying, except, of course, when heroines are so lifeless and conventional as to evoke simply and automatically approving response. Austen is very conscious that an honest (not stock) response to perfection is likely to be annoyance and spite rather than emulation – unless the pictures of perfection are handled brilliantly, as she does Mr Knightley in *Emma,* her attractive and completely successful 'answer' to Richardson's inhumanly perfect Sir

Charles Grandison. By implication, in this letter to her niece and in her novels, Austen criticizes popular notions of the way readers respond to fiction. In the creation of her own fiction, she discards naïve assumptions about readers' responses to literature, although she respects the naïveté of readers who do not wish their 'amiable and delicate' sentiments tampered with. She does not address herself to these readers. As she says, they should read no more.

With equal force, Austen rejects eighteenth-century fiction which pretends to educate the emotions by indulging them. The sentimental novel rendered emotion, particularly distress, in order to provide the reader with opportunities for sympathy, then considered the great enlarger of the human spirit. The didactic aim of this fiction descended readily to a cult of display in which the author and audience collaborated. One contemporary reader has recorded that, when she read Henry Mackenzie's *The Man of Feeling,* 'as I was a girl of fourteen not yet versed in sentiment, I had a secret dread I should not cry enough to gain the credit of proper sensibility'.[20] At fifteen, Austen's criticism of the sentimental novel was so acute that she could write the hilarious burlesque, 'Love and Freindship'. In *Sense and Sensibility,* she gives shape to her mature criticism of sentimental convention and reveals her conviction that literature is not meant to offer or to encourage easy opportunities for sympathy. The reader's propensity to feel for Marianne Dashwood in preference to her sister Elinor is exposed and combatted. At the same time, Austen recognizes that in life and in literature, certain easy responses must (or at least may) prevail: wit, charm, openness, confidence, energy and good looks will guarantee favourable or sympathetic responses wherever they appear, for these attractions are powerful enough to suspend or disarm judgment. Instead of deploring, like a moralizer, these truths about sympathy and judgment, she learns to exploit them in her novels to help create the more complex and sensitive responses she requires. Although she is fully aware of the recalcitrance of the average reader, she intends and designs her novels to exercise and challenge his responses. He is asked to produce more intricate, more complex and, sometimes, more unconventional responses than he may be prepared for.

In obtaining these responses, Austen is a manipulator, but in no negative sense. She manipulates her readers' responses to didactic and moral ends. Her power to do so arises both from her highly sophisticated awareness of readers' probable responses to fiction as well as from her increasing mastery of technique. At the same time, her power to evoke and to manipulate response is not tyrannical: she does not harass the reader or bully him. He feels her power only if he pays close attention, and Austen does not make the explicit or obtrusive demands upon a reader's attention typical of even the great novelists of the eighteenth century, Richardson, Fielding and Sterne. She practices an emotional didacticism which her contemporaries and even her greatest predecessors often sought and missed: a refining that amounts to an educating of judgment and sympathy.

Such manipulation of response underlies all Austen's novels except *Northanger Abbey*. In it, Austen limits herself to the two responses of suspense and distress which Gothic and sentimental novels were designed to obtain from their readers. She first exposes everything false and absurd in the conventions these novels rely on to elicit suspense and distress, and then surprises her readers by using the conventions more successfully than her predecessors did, to evoke the same responses. By this means, Austen shows her own power over her readers at the same time that she reveals a shrewd consciousness that, in literature as in life, the simplest emotional responses are among the most powerful and also among the most readily obtained, even from readers who have been taught to laugh at them.

Austen's interests in *Northanger Abbey* are comic more than didactic. In *Sense and Sensibility* her didactic intentions mature. She addresses herself to the moral and emotional responses of judgment and sympathy rather than to the parallel and simpler responses of suspense and distress, and she develops techniques which will educate her readers' responses. The joke on the relation between literature and life which the narrator in *Northanger Abbey* never stops playing on the reader and on Catherine Morland is in *Sense and Sensibility* assimilated to character. Partly as a result, Marianne is a heroine as Catherine cannot be. Her faults of conduct, feeling and judgment cause serious consequences for herself and others as Catherine's do not. To allow these consequences to be registered, Austen employs a technique she never afterwards relinquishes, the technique of contrast. She constructs among the feelings, judgments, predicaments and conduct of all her characters parallels and contrasts so elaborate and insistent that the reader cannot escape comparing, weighing and evaluating. Austen further assists this process by allowing the characters themselves to weigh and evaluate their own conduct, feelings and judgments.

Nevertheless, the central issue of *Sense and Sensibility* is not really discussed by the characters. The reader is left to infer and decide it himself. This issue is, what kind of judgment and what degree of sympathy to accord Elinor and Marianne? Austen intends that the reader's inclination to be charmed by Marianne and to be alienated by Elinor should be subtly redirected by the text. Unfortunately, the 'romantic' presuppositions about emotion and its expression which permit Marianne to disregard Elinor's feelings are still prevalent enough to have encouraged many modern readers to be as unjust to Elinor as Marianne is. Their injustice fully attests the unruliness of judgment and sympathy, acknowledged and exposed by Austen in *Sense and Sensibility* even as she attempts to correct it in her readers.

As responses to literature and to life, judgment and sympathy are not merely more significant than the suspense and distress examined in *Northanger Abbey*: they are immeasurably more complex and intractable. Recognizing this, Austen continues to refine and to extend her techniques for exercising the reader's responses. *Pride and Prejudice* therefore occupies an especially significant place in her development. It is a completely successful and even triumphant achievement in itself. It effects a transition between the concerns, themes and techniques of Austen's own early novels and the more difficult and subtle ones of *Mansfield Park, Emma* and *Persuasion*. And, finally, its relations to Burney's *Cecilia* and Richardson's *Sir Charles Grandison* show why Austen liked these novelists so well and what she learned from them.

Austen's admiration for *Cecilia* and particularly for *Grandison* is well documented but largely unaccountable to most critics, who content themselves with a few remarks in passing. Yet *Pride and Prejudice* assimilates the design of *Cecilia* (an attempt to examine, in a comic, non-epistolary narrative, 'how differently pride ... operates upon different minds')[21] and the central concern of *Grandison* (an attempt to manipulate and educate the reader's first impressions of character) to the theme first sounded in *Sense and Sensibility*: the attempt to educate judgment and sympathy. The intentions of *Pride and Prejudice* are far more complex than those of any previous Austen novel, and its techniques necessarily reflect this greater complexity. In *Pride and Prejudice*, Austen exploits even more fully the technique of contrast which sufficed for the themes of *Sense and Sensibility,* and she adopts or develops in addition certain other techniques visible in *Cecilia* and *Grandison*.

One such technique deserves special consideration. Both *Cecilia* and *Grandison* show traces of an overall structural principle which I call 'linear irony': the action is organized so as to reverse or undercut the main characters' expectations or judgments and the reader's as well.[22] The importance of linear irony to the structure of *Pride and Prejudice* cannot be exaggerated. The reversal in Elizabeth's opinion of Darcy which provides the novel's obvious and overall structure also provides details in structure, for Elizabeth's judgments are reversed or undercut throughout. Elizabeth's wit and charm are so disarming, however, that the reader is likely to acquiesce in her mistaken judgments, although certainly he is not forced to do so. In this way, the technique of linear irony systematically organizes the action of *Pride and Prejudice* so as to engage, test and chasten the reader's judgment without actually misleading him.

To define the influence of Burney and Richardson upon Austen may seem to require a study of the social comedy of all three, for it is often supposed that Austen's comedy of manners is anticipated by the earlier novelists. Upon examination, however, Austen's use of the comedy of manners in *Pride and Prejudice,* the first of her novels to employ this convention fully, greatly extends and refines even that of Richardson in *Grandison,* particularly in the use of wit and dialogue. In *Pride and Prejudice,* Austen finds that wit and dialogue can be effective means to control and complicate her readers' responses (especially to Elizabeth, Mr Bennet, Wickham and Darcy). These terms are distinct. Some of the characters' wit in *Pride and Prejudice* does not really occur in dialogue (which implies exchange or reciprocity) but in isolation. Mr Bennet's wit is often isolated from dialogue in this sense. Admittedly, like Austen in her treatment of Mr Bennet, Richardson can make his characters' wit attract the reader and repel him alternately, for wit is one of his devices for manipulating his readers' impressions. Nevertheless, Richardson does not really anticipate in *Grandison* the sense of play and sense of structure which permit the wit and dialogue of *Pride and Prejudice* to serve the themes so brilliantly. Similarly, neither Richardson nor Austen herself in *Sense and Sensibility* anticipates one of the most important discoveries of *Pride and Prejudice,* one Austen never loses sight of afterward: the discovery that the characters themselves can debate as well as dramatize the central issues, to excellent effect. The central issue of *Pride and Prejudice* is the process of judging and evaluating character, and the characters talk about this process while it is actually occurring.

These new techniques allow Austen a treatment of Elizabeth Bennet and of the reader which exposes the fallibility of judgment and humbles pride in it, while insisting that it be exercised nonetheless. Linear irony, especially, depends for its effect on engaged, not suspended, judgment, and all Austen's techniques deliberately make suspension of judgment difficult. The structures which contain the comedy of manners undermine those impressions and judgments which the comedy has invited. The reader's judgment is as chastened at the end as Elizabeth's.

Yet this subversive treatment of judgment is not cynical. Elizabeth's pride of judgment is humbled, as is the reader's, but judgment is educated and refined in the process. And however serious the issues, the tone is genial. In *Pride and Prejudice,* Austen succeeds brilliantly (where her contemporaries or predecessors succeed partially or fail miserably) in delighting and instructing the reader. The themes and techniques of *Pride and Prejudice* accomplish their eighteenth-century didactic end, moral and emotional instruction, at the same time that they create a degree of intimacy with the characters and an absorption in the world of the novel surpassed only by the reader's response to the novels which follow it, *Mansfield Park, Emma* and *Persuasion.* The methods of *Pride and Prejudice* are essentially those of the later novels. Although Austen refines these methods so as to create more powerful and profound effects, once the themes, techniques and intentions of *Pride and Prejudice* are understood, those of the later novels become accessible.

This account of Austen's early novels as intending to manipulate and educate her readers' responses, and as developing increasingly sophisticated means to do so, runs counter to some modern assumptions about literature. The classical dictum, still operative in eighteenth- and early nineteenth-century fiction, that literature should delight and instruct, has since been largely abandoned or qualified beyond recognition, and few words used in criticism carry more negative connotations than 'didactic'. Perhaps for this reason, although Austen's powers to delight are almost universally acknowledged, her successfully didactic methods and intentions are now seldom claimed. Sometimes they are even resented when discovered. A hostility to these intentions, resulting in obliviousness, is perfectly illustrated when Andrew Wright asks: if Marianne Dashwood 'is meant merely to exemplify an unlaudable predisposition to "enthusiasm", why is she so lovable? Why, indeed, is she not portrayed as an Isabella Thorpe?'[23] This recalcitrance in some of her critics fully attests that Austen is dealing with responses to literature and to life which require some refinement. That her methods can baffle even trained, well-disposed, and sensitive readers of her fiction so that they misjudge her characters and mistake her intentions because of their own prejudices is an absurdity that Austen's novels were designed to anticipate and to combat, but which she would nevertheless have enjoyed.

1 *Northanger Abbey*

Austen's earliest novel, *Northanger Abbey* (1803; published 1818), is by far the most 'bookish'. Written in response to contemporary fiction, it exhibits the most visibly comic relation to that fiction of all Austen's full-length works. It insists on pointing up, and treating comically, the incongruities between literature and life, and the tendencies of novels to imitate each other rather than life. In this sense, *Northanger Abbey* is a novel about writing novels, even an 'anti-novel', as long as these terms imply no portentousness and allow Austen to delight in, and occasionally to exploit, the conventions she exposes and parodies. Later, in *Sense and Sensibility* and *Pride and Prejudice,* allusions to the conventions of contemporary fiction will be equally pervasive, but less obvious and more fully absorbed. Some conventions, especially structural ones, will simply be appropriated (courtship ending in marriage, two central contrasting female characters). Others, Austen will learn to use as one means to complicate and manipulate her readers' responses to the characters: witness the problems for interpretation caused in *Sense and Sensibility* by Marianne Dashwood, who is a highly conventional character both in that her tastes, judgments and behaviour are governed by established modes of sensibility, and in that she shares this quality with many other contemporary heroines. Austen's later novels include, then, some serious uses for literary conventions. In *Northanger Abbey,* however, comic, flamboyant and even outrageous allusions to books and their conventions are the rule.[1]

Several literary references in the first chapter proclaim that the relation between literature and life will be a major concern, and further, that this relation will depend on an inversion: the events, anticipations, responses and qualities that are ordinary in life become extraordinary in fiction:

> No one who had ever seen Catherine Morland in her infancy, would have supposed her born to be an heroine. . . . She was fond of all boys' plays, and greatly preferred cricket not merely to dolls, but to the more heroic enjoyments of infancy, nursing a dormouse, feeding a canary-bird, or watering a rosebush. Indeed she had no taste for a garden; and if she gathered flowers at all, it was chiefly for the pleasure of mischief

11

– at least so it was conjectured from her always preferring those which she was forbidden to take. –Such were her propensities – her abilities were quite as extraordinary. She never could learn or understand any thing before she was taught; and sometimes not even then, for she was often inattentive, and occasionally stupid (13–14).

This joke on literature and life, once announced, is never allowed to drop, however it is developed or transformed. Each succeeding chapter insists on repeating or extending the joke or (more respectably) theme, and theories which conjecture that the Gothic parody was interpolated at a later date fail to reckon with this insistence.

A theme so clear and so loudly proclaimed ought to make *Northanger Abbey* the simplest and most lucid of Austen's works – yet critics do disagree, if not about the presence of the theme, then about its execution. Clearly, difficulties must arise for an author who handles such a theme: an anti-novel must be a novel nonetheless, an anti-heroine a heroine still; and rejecting or ridiculing one set of conventions entails adopting another set. Each of these paradoxes poses a separable critical problem, though all are closely related. The first becomes the problem of whether the Bath sections and the 'Gothic' or Abbey sections are unified; the second, whether Catherine's character is interesting or developed enough; the third, whether the melodramatic climax of the plot (General Tilney's expelling Catherine from the Abbey) and its resolution are credible or acceptable. Critics disagree both in their estimations of Austen's success in dealing with each of these problems, and in the importance they attach to each.

1. CRITICAL PROBLEMS

The credibility and development of Catherine's character are issues very intimately connected with the problem of unity. If Catherine matures at Bath, then how can she be so gullible at Northanger? Does she mature at Bath, or is she intended to be merely functional, serving the themes rather than developing as a character? Critics who see Catherine as inconsistent or undeveloped usually find the Bath and Northanger sections discontinuous, and the latter dissatisfying. Those who detect an educative or maturing process are generally satisfied with the novel. But attempts to confirm or deny the coherence of Catherine's character are equally futile. Between her character at Bath and at Northanger no clear dividing line may be drawn and no consistent development traced. Austen's interests in Catherine, and in the novel, lie elsewhere.

However Catherine's character is assessed, nothing so strenuous is demanded of it as is required of General Tilney's: his character moves the plot, providing the climax and resolution. At least one of Austen's contemporaries balked at this. Maria Edgeworth wrote to her aunt, 'The behavior of the General in "Northanger Abbey," packing off the young lady without a servant or the common civilities which any bear of a man, not to say gentleman, would have shown, is quite outrageously out of drawing and out of nature.'[2] Modern critics who discuss the General's character agree, though in different terms. Most discussions of his role in the novel, however, are concerned with the effect of his actions on the theme, not with their (or his) credibility. Irony has, after all, supplanted Edgeworth's 'nature' as a literary desideratum, and critics who find in the climax a crowning irony are not lacking. A. Walton Litz comments representatively, 'Catherine's belief in a violent and uncertain life lurking beneath the surface of English society is nearer the truth than the complacent conviction, shared by the readers of Mrs Radcliffe, that life in the Home Counties is always sane and orderly.... Jane Austen's irony is not directed at Catherine's sympathetic imagination, but at her misuse of it; and the novel's deepest criticism is reserved for the average reader's complacent reaction to the exposure of Catherine's "folly." '[3]

Readers who wish to find explicit moral norms within the text, rather than irony, are, on the other hand, disturbed by the climax. Kenneth Moler considers Henry's stance a norm which the climax contradicts, and he rejects the ironic interpretation as a possible way out of the difficulty: 'There does not seem to be the slightest indication that the general's conduct is designed to undermine the novel's assertion that common sense such as Henry's leads to the maximum possible amount of clear-sightedness.'[4]

The different problems isolated by the critics, and their different stances, do not preclude agreement on two fundamental issues: approaching *Northanger Abbey,* and ranking it in relation to Austen's other works. With few exceptions, critics assign it the lowest rank, while appreciating its freshness and finding in it many hints or anticipations of later style, treatment, themes, characters and dialogue. Certainly these hints can be pointed out when searched for; nevertheless, to approach *Northanger Abbey* in this way, with expectations and standards created by the other novels, is not entirely revealing or just and inevitably entails critical views as widely diverging as those cited. The differences between *Northanger Abbey* and the later novels are far more significant than any similarities or parallels, though these do exist. They are particularly evident when Austen momentarily suspends her mockery of literary conventions in order to mock the insipid social conventions of Bath: its balls (Catherine's first visit to the Upper Rooms is especially appalling), its Sunday promenades, and above all its conversation, explicitly ridiculed by Henry Tilney: 'After chatting some time on such matters as naturally arose from the objects around them, he suddenly addressed her with – "I have hitherto been very remiss, madam, in the proper attentions of a partner here; I have not yet asked you how long you have been in Bath; whether you were ever here before; whether you have been at the Upper Rooms, the theatre, and the concert; and how you like the place altogether"' (25). More important, *Northanger Abbey* is full of jokes about judgments like those central to the later novels: 'Catherine was complimented out of further bitterness. Frederick could not be unpardonably guilty, while Henry made himself so agreeable' (219). Finding such likenesses offers no clue as to what Austen is actually doing, however, and in fact obscures it. The differences between *Northanger Abbey* and the other novels are far more illuminating and must be explored if her intentions are to be defined. To do this will not reverse the judgment already pronounced. From any approach, *Northanger Abbey* remains the least satisfying of Austen's novels, and the slightest in emotional and moral content. It is so, however, with a purpose. *Northanger Abbey* intentionally differs from the five other novels in almost every possible way.

2. *NORTHANGER ABBEY* AND THE LATER NOVELS

The major difference has already been suggested and can be expressed readily enough: *Northanger Abbey* is simply comic and lacks most of the moral concerns and discriminations of the other Austen novels. This difference extends to the character of the hero, Henry Tilney. No other Austen hero is so superior in wit to the heroine, and yet it is difficult to claim that he educates Catherine in anything but a greater consciousness of convention. He does not supply a moral standard which the heroine must learn to accept or move toward, as Emma moves toward Mr Knightley's. Nor is he in need of any enlightenment or reformation parallel to the heroine's, as Mr Darcy is. His function instead is to make jokes about literary and social convention. He is alive to all clichés of feeling and language, and his insistence on using words discriminatingly is relentless but hardly 'moral'. He teaches Catherine about using words like 'faithful' (196), 'torment' (109) and 'nice' (108) inaccurately, but only accuracy is at stake: when Catherine remarks, 'I really thought

before, young men despised novels amazingly', he replies, 'It is
amazingly; it may well suggest *amazement* if they do – for they read nearly
as many as women' (107). All his corrections are made in the same tone
and are thus utterly lacking in the emotional and moral resonance of Mr
Knightley's response to Emma's describing Frank Churchill as amiable.
When he rejects that description, he vents his jealousy and at the same
time uses the words 'amiable' and 'aimable' to make a distinction
between manners and morals: 'No, Emma, your amiable young man can
be amiable only in French, not in English. He may be very "aimable,"
have very good manners, and be very agreeable; but he can have no
English delicacy towards the feelings of other people: nothing really
amiable about him' (149). Even if Catherine can be said to learn anything
from Henry, it does not amount to a moral growth of any kind. For once,
Austen fails to accord a moral dimension to the mastery of social (and in
this case, literary) convention.

Other techniques and qualities usually associated with Austen are also
conspicuously absent in *Northanger Abbey*. It has, for instance, fewer
major characters than any other Austen novel, with the result that the
parallels and contrasts between characters, so extensive and so carefully
exploited later, are perfunctory or simply lacking. Similarly, dialogue in
Northanger Abbey does not try for the complex effects achieved later; no
speeches convey feelings or motives more complicated than Isabella's, and
none are conveyed more subtly. When Catherine reveals her infatuation
for Henry, she sounds very like Isabella herself, although her transparency
springs from artlessness and Isabella's from 'shallow artifice' (218).
Catherine inquires, 'Was not the young lady he danced with on Monday
a Miss Smith?' and Miss Tilney replies:

'Yes, an acquaintance of Mrs Hughes.'
'I dare say she was very glad to dance. Do you think her pretty?'
'Not very.'
'He never comes to the Pump-room, I suppose?' (73).

Much of the dialogue is like this, 'broad' (Austen's own term)[5] rather
than revealing. Even Henry's irony is often similarly broad, especially
juxtaposed with Catherine's literalness; and during one of the few times
he is serious, that is, when he first indicates to the reader his own feelings
for Catherine, he provides a measure of Austen's unconcern in this novel
with subtly revealing dialogue. Catherine has explained her seeming
rudeness in driving off when she was engaged to walk with him and with
his sister, and although he has become cordial again, for Catherine

yet a something of solicitude remained, from which sprang thè following question, thoroughly artless in itself, though rather distressing to the gentleman: – 'But, Mr Tilney, why were *you* less generous than your sister? If she felt such confidence in my good intentions, and could suppose it to be only a mistake, why should *you* be so ready to take offence?'
'Me! – I take offence!'
'Nay, I am sure by your look, when you came into the box, you were angry.'
'I angry! I could have no right.'
'Well, nobody would have thought you had no right who saw your face.' He replied by asking her to make room for him, and talking of the play (94–5).

Even the comedy in *Northanger Abbey* is simple, in the sense of lacking in development, by comparison with the later novels. Austen shows no interest in obtaining through careful repetition the cumulative comic effects achieved elsewhere. Mrs Allen's repeated 'wish of a numerous acquaintance in Bath' (25) is, once voiced, merely referred to at the start of two succeeding chapters; it has none of the comic, or even explosive, force of assertive, immutable human idiocy which distinguishes Mrs Bennet's whines over the entail of Longbourn and Mrs Norris's outbursts of indignation over the large dining table at Mansfield parsonage.

Catherine's character, however, sets *Northanger Abbey* most completely apart from the comic techniques and concern with moral judgments which mark the other novels. The critical dispute, impossible elsewhere, over whether she matures or not is symptomatic of the futility of approaching her character with expectations created by other Austen heroines. She does not live in the complicated world of moral perception and moral choice that they inhabit. Although she is often required to choose, both the choices and their consequences are usually treated only comically. They are not felt, nor meant to be: witness the unlucky decision to drive with John Thorpe and consequent failure to walk with the Tilneys. The narrator is first rather heavily ironic about Catherine's distress: 'And now I may dismiss my heroine to the sleepless couch, which is the true heroine's portion; to a pillow strewed with thorns and wet with tears. And lucky may she think herself, if she get another good night's rest in the course of the next three months' (90). Catherine is then conducted to a play the next evening, where 'the comedy so well suspended her care, that no one, observing her during the first four acts, would have supposed she had any wretchedness about her' (92). The grief which follows with the fifth act, of seeing Henry cold to her, is meant to be amusing only: 'Catherine was restlessly miserable; she could almost have run round to the box in which he sat, and forced him to hear her explanation' (93). Despite her naïveté and gullibility, Catherine chooses well and behaves well in all important respects, like Elinor Dashwood, Fanny Price and Anne Elliot. Their good behaviour, however, is often accompanied by some considerable cost to themselves. The reader is meant to feel their doubts or anxieties over their own judgments and actions, as well as their sufferings. By comparison, Catherine's good behaviour is effortless. Her doubts and anxieties are always treated comically and her distress nearly always, until the end when she is expelled from Northanger and some sustained misery is registered.

Catherine's remaining differences from the other heroines could, for the most part, be induced from the one already mentioned. Just as Austen shows no interest in placing Catherine within a complex world of moral perceptions and judgments, she neglects to provide for her the elaborate, fully-imagined and realized social world of the other heroines. Catherine is merely sketched in relation to her family, for instance; we know few of her nine brothers and sisters, and four names are not even supplied. Such sketchiness would be unthinkable in any of the other novels, where each of the heroines' homes is present to the imagination without being described in detail, and where the families of each are delineated, occasionally down to remote connections. Charlotte Heywood, the heroine of the unfinished novel *Sanditon* (1817), is the only other central character portrayed as sketchily as Catherine. *Sanditon,* in fact, can be considered a re-thinking of *Northanger Abbey,* an attempt to combine the freshness and burlesque energy of the latter with the explorations of emotional and moral responsiveness characteristic of the other novels.

Northanger Abbey is not entirely unconcerned with the judgments characters make of each other; rather, the distinct nature of its concern must be registered. Catherine is notorious, certainly, for her hilariously poor judgment of Isabella Thorpe – for taking Isabella at her own valuation and for believing all her professions of affection. This flagrant error somewhat obscures Catherine's capacity to estimate other characters correctly, even shrewdly. One of the difficulties encountered in claiming that Catherine matures is, in fact, that she is capable of certain discriminations from the start. When she first meets Henry Tilney, she detects his foible despite being attracted to him, a feat none of Austen's other heroines accomplish: 'Catherine feared ... that he indulged himself a little too much with the foibles of others' (29). Later, when Henry appears, thanks to Catherine's literalness, to have been rude to his sister ('she is by no means a simpleton in general'), 'Catherine looked grave' (113). Austen is poking fun at her solemnity, but the indicated readiness to judge is not isolated. Despite her literalness, she does not credit Anne Thorpe's professed happiness at being excluded from the drive to Clifton (115), nor, more important, John Thorpe's affection for her: 'She was almost as far from believing as from wishing it to be sincere'. Catherine's mixture of naïveté and shrewdness is perfectly illustrated by the rest of the passage:

> she had not forgotten that [John Thorpe] could mistake, and his assertion of the offer and of her encouragement convinced her that his mistakes could sometimes be very egregious. In vanity therefore she gained but little, her chief profit was in wonder. That he should think it worth his while to fancy himself in love with her, was a matter of lively astonishment. Isabella talked of his attentions; *she* had never been sensible of any; but Isabella had said many things which she hoped had been spoken in haste, and would never be said again; and upon this she was glad to rest altogether for present ease and comfort (148).

These reflections occur before Catherine leaves Bath, and provide one of several indications that any reading of her development as continuous is untenable, however attractive. Catherine's earliest ingenuousness does not desert her even after her Gothic illusions are dispelled and she has learned through James's letter that Isabella is mercenary. She still believes General Tilney is not mercenary simply because he says so and in spite of his children's different opinion: his 'generous and disinterested sentiments on the subject of money ... tempted her to think his disposition in such matters misunderstood by his children' (208). Austen is simply not interested in showing a consistent or continuous development in Catherine's judgment or in her character. She prefers to call upon Catherine's shrewdness and her naïveté alternately, depending on which will create the most unexpected or incongruous effect. Catherine is comic throughout. Austen keeps up the joke of a naïve, not unintelligent, good-natured character who cannot detect artifice, who almost always takes everything at face value: irony, insincerity and even novels. The situation created is conventional, but not often treated principally for comedy. Moler notes that 'the naive young person in eighteenth- and early nineteenth-century literature is often a reproach to the folly and vice of the sophisticated society into which he is introduced'.[6] Nevertheless, both the theme (naïveté operating in a vulgar or sophisticated circle) and its essentially comic treatment in *Northanger*

Abbey have analogues. The theme is central to Burney's *Evelina* (1778), and brilliantly inverted in Henry James's *The Europeans* (1878), where sophistication is utterly disarmed by being placed in naive circle. Like *Northanger Abbey*, both novels exploit the comic possibilities of the situation in preference to its moral ones, though both authors later reverse themselves in order to emphasize moral implications over comic effects, Burney rather clumsily in *Camilla: or, a Picture of Youth* (1796), but James magnificently in *What Maisie Knew* (1897), where this theme certainly receives its most profound and moving development.

Austen herself loses interest in the theme after *Northanger Abbey*; at least, she never again chooses to construct a novel in which the heroine's judgments are so naïve and, whether correct or incorrect, have so little moral or emotional resonance. Later heroines will pride themselves on their judgments, like Elizabeth Bennet and Emma Woodhouse – and very unlike Catherine – and will suffer some humiliation in consequence; or they will judge correctly but suffer for it in various ways – equally unlike Catherine. These differences are characteristic and pervasive, and reflect an enormous distinction in conception, technique and final effect. In the later novels, each character and each scene must be weighed in relation to the rest. Even in *Sense and Sensibility,* every major effect is cumulative. *Northanger Abbey,* on the other hand, obtains its effects almost entirely by reversing the reader's expectations relentlessly and outrageously, by administering continual rude shocks which, however, are felt only in relation to the ones immediately preceding and following, each shock cancelling the one before instead of adding to it. *Northanger Abbey* is one-dimensional, without the flimsiness that implies: immediacy, excitement and thrust are achieved and do in some degree compensate for losses in sustained or accumulated power.

3. THE INTENTIONS OF *NORTHANGER ABBEY*

The question remains, why does Austen choose to write a novel like *Northanger Abbey*? This question entails a number of others. First, if Catherine and the novel itself can be faulted by so many critics for failing to develop coherently, and for existing merely as vehicles for the author's burlesque intentions, then perhaps these intentions will bear closer examination. What are Austen's designs on her readers? Specifically, does she use burlesque to manipulate her readers in any way, beyond that already mentioned: jolting them, frustrating or confounding their expectations of a novel (which is something she will always do, though less violently)? If these further or larger designs exist, how significant or successful can they be if they have remained unobserved by her critics – by her readers, in other words?

In general, critics have not neglected the burlesque elements in *Northanger Abbey*. They point out the conventions mocked and suggest possible models; they note the degree to which Austen's burlesque is superior to her contemporaries', lighter, more charming and more amusing; and they note the contributions of burlesque to the theme of the novel and to its statements on art and life. Their study ought to be exhaustive, then, but is not, probably because at the same time the burlesque elements are felt to be excrescences, hiding or obscuring or sometimes quite obliterating what interests the critics more: character development, social comedy, mastery of dialogue. As a result, Austen's interests can be partially overlooked, particularly in the Gothic burlesque.

Both genres burlesqued, the sentimental novel and its Gothic offshoot, are now felt to be so ridiculous and so remote from life that exploding them seems gratuitous; but the sentimental burlesque is better received and more discussed, no doubt because it allows (or at any rate does not prevent) the social comedy and satire which the 'Gothic interlude' at Northanger is thought to interrupt. And it is true that if Austen were merely mocking the absurdities of these genres, or pointing out that Gothic and sentimental novels do or do not have any relation to life, then the burlesque elements in *Northanger Abbey* would have received all the attention they could deserve. But she does more than this. She explores the emotional basis or appeal of sentimental and Gothic fiction, although not simply 'to expose both its basic sentimentality and fundamental unreality', as Litz claims when speaking of the 'Radcliffean novel'.[7] It would be neat and satisfying but equally inaccurate to say instead that she discovers and exploits whatever may be genuine or moving in either genre. She does, but incidentally; such discoveries do not seem to be her main concern. Her real interest is, evidently, more playful: she wants to bring off a *tour de force*, to expose her readers to everything absurd in a convention or genre and then to make the convention 'work' all the same. She explodes a convention and then exploits it, and in doing so, often succeeds in eliciting a response from the reader in spite of himself. In the later novels too she attempts to elicit responses which go against the grain, but there her purpose is didactic: she is educating the reader to produce somewhat more complex responses than he may be used to or care for. In *Northanger Abbey*, however, she demonstrates the force of literary convention, its fundamental accommodation and appeal to human emotions – but she also simply shows off her power over her readers.[8]

4. MANIPULATION OF SENTIMENTAL CONVENTION

In dealing with the emotions which underlie sentimental conventions, Austen is on the whole less bold and less successful in her designs on her readers than she is in her treatment of Gothic conventions, perhaps because sentimental conventions may be further removed than Gothic ones from genuine feelings. By far the most characteristic feature, amounting to a convention, of the sentimental novel was 'distress'. As Tompkins has noted, ' "Distress" was a technical term in criticism, and authors set themselves . . . to get the heroine to the point when she finds herself penniless in a hackney-coach in London, with nowhere to drive to, with a rising fever and an injured reputation'.[9] Falsity and absurdity underlie the convention, for unnatural, strained behaviour (often called 'delicacy') is invariably required to produce and sustain the 'distress', and only Richardson in *Clarissa* could sufficiently motivate and justify such behaviour. Austen very neatly and very consistently burlesques this convention in *Northanger Abbey*; she treats Catherine's 'heroic' distresses comically, so much so, that Catherine's distress at Northanger comes as a shock, and is meant to.

Austen's methods of preparing this shock are worth examining. From the start, she takes every opportunity to mock and deflate the conventional distresses of novel heroines, beginning with Catherine's 'false position' at a ball; she is engaged to dance with John Thorpe, but he doesn't appear:

as the real dignity of her situation could not be known, she was sharing with the scores of other young ladies still sitting down all the discredit of wanting a partner. To be disgraced in the eye of the world, to wear the appearance of infamy while her heart is all purity, her actions all innocence, and the misconduct of another the true source of her debasement, is one of those circumstances which peculiarly belong to the heroine's life, and her fortitude under it what particularly dignifies her character. Catherine had fortitude too; she suffered, but no murmur passed her lips (53).

Here Catherine does play a conventional heroine's part, but the part and its trials and sufferings are deflated and trivialized. The next occasion for distress is somewhat more serious, though equally conventional, and Catherine's role is in this case anti-heroic. When Henry is cold to her at the play, having evidently misjudged her (a situation highly favoured by Austen's predecessors, especially Burney), 'Feelings rather natural than heroic possessed her; instead of considering her own dignity injured by this ready condemnation – instead of proudly resolving, in conscious innocence, to shew her resentment towards him who could harbour a doubt of it, to leave to him all the trouble of seeking an explanation, and to enlighten him on the past only by avoiding his sight, or flirting with somebody else, she took to herself all the shame of misconduct, or at least of its appearance, and was only eager for an opportunity of explaining its cause' (93). And Catherine does explain herself to Henry almost immediately.

Austen has exposed here what is false and absurd in the sentimental novel's convention of distress by the device of substituting life for literature, and 'natural' for 'heroic' responses. Again and again, the narrator points the contrast between 'natural' and conventional responses, between 'common feelings of common life' and 'the refined susceptibilities, the tender emotions' of sentimental fiction (19) or between 'The anxieties of common life' and the 'alarms of romance' (201). But even this obsessive concern cannot quite account for Austen's choosing to duplicate, in the very next chapter (XIII), the incidents which led to Catherine's explanation and self-justification at the play. In Chapter XI, John Thorpe persuades Catherine to drive with him by telling her he saw the Tilneys drive out of town, so that she cannot possibly keep her engagement to walk with them. In Chapter XII, Catherine has the opportunity at the play to explain to Henry her seeming rudeness in not keeping her engagement. In Chapter XIII, Catherine has once more engaged herself to walk with the Tilneys, and refuses a drive to Clifton with her brother and the Thorpes. John Thorpe tries to force her to go by telling the Tilneys that she will walk with them another time, for she has recollected a prior engagement to drive to Clifton. Catherine runs after the Tilneys to explain, and to reconfirm the original plan. The duplication is almost exact, and is thus especially puzzling; what can this second incident add to the novel? Conventional heroic delicacy has already been completely parodied. Catherine's steadiness, her determination and power to do right, and her willingness to explain herself have all been established. And the Thorpes' selfishness and unscrupulousness surely need no further development.

The difference between the two incidents, and the reason for the second, lies in tone. The second incident is treated more seriously than the first, though still comically. It lacks the constant broadly ironic reminders of what a heroine's behaviour ought to be. Instead, Catherine is briefly allowed to be a heroine. She is under pressure from the Thorpes and from her brother to change her mind and to do something she thinks is wrong.

When she resists, they are angry, she is distressed, and her distress is registered, though with some traces of irony at Catherine's expense in the clichés used ('hearts at war', 'heart swelled'):

> The three others still continued together, walking in a most uncomfortable manner to poor Catherine; sometimes not a word was said, sometimes she was again attacked with supplications or reproaches, and her arm was still linked within Isabella's, though their hearts were at war. At one moment she was softened, at another irritated; always distressed, but always steady.
>
> 'I did not think you had been so obstinate, Catherine,' said James; 'you were not used to be so hard to persuade; you once were the kindest, best-tempered of my sisters.'
>
> 'I hope I am not less so now,' she replied, very feelingly; 'but indeed I cannot go. If I am wrong, I am doing what I believe to be right.'
>
> 'I suspect,' said Isabella, in a low voice, 'there is no great struggle.'
>
> Catherine's heart swelled; she drew away her arm, and Isabella made no opposition (99-100).

Catherine's steadiness here helps give the scene an emotional content much greater and more felt than is usual in *Northanger Abbey*, and yet neither moral growth in Catherine nor a moral choice is at issue. Instead, Austen seems, in a rather uncertain way, to be playing with her readers. She treats Catherine's distress and the situation causing it first in a wholly comic and parodic manner, and once she has thus convinced her readers that novelistic distress of the conventional sort has no real foundation in human behaviour or emotion, or at all events that such distress will not be found in *her* novel, she loses no time in making just such distress felt, both by her heroine and by her readers. If this is her design, however, she does not insist on it. As Catherine runs after the Tilneys and finally runs up the stairs in their lodgings, distance is gained in every sense. Comedy supplants distress:

> Then, opening the first door before her, which happened to be the right, she immediately found herself in the drawing-room with General Tilney, his son and daughter. Her explanation, defective only in being - from her irritation of nerves and shortness of breath - no explanation at all, was instantly given. 'I am come in a great hurry - It was all a mistake - I never promised to go - I told them from the first I could not go. - I ran away in a great hurry to explain it. - I did not care what you thought of me. - I would not stay for the servant' (102).

Comedy is re-established so quickly that the shock of Catherine's being actually in real distress has scarcely time to be felt; this is not so at the novel's climax (when Catherine is thrown out of Northanger), which comes also as the climax to Austen's treatment of sentimental convention. This climax is more clearly and intentionally shocking, for Austen has very carefully left the reader wholly unprepared for it. Not only has she previously done everything to minimize Catherine's distresses and to establish the unlikelihood of her suffering a heroine's trials, but she has also included an early prediction of this particular trial, designed to convince the reader to expect no such thing. When Captain Tilney is introduced, the reader is assured that '*He* cannot be the instigator of the three villains in horsemen's great coats, by whom she will hereafter be forced into a travelling-chaise and four, which will drive off with incredible speed' (131). The reader is surely left, like Catherine, 'undisturbed by presentiments of such an evil' (131), and yet the evil actually and almost literally occurs. Possibly, then, the critical dispute over the credibility or significance of this climax is beside the point. Austen intentionally sacrifices credibility in General Tilney's character in order to make the climax more shocking; the climax is meant to shock, meant to create in the reader those responses of sympathy and concern that the conventional distress of a sentimental heroine was supposed to excite, but with a difference. The self-indulgent tears, the 'refined susceptibilities, the tender emotions' of sentimental fiction are neither evoked in the reader nor displayed by the heroine. In fact, the narrator carefully points out that Catherine's own responses to this catastrophe are free from self-conscious, sentimental or Gothic exaggeration and heightening, and no doubt Austen expects her readers to imitate Catherine in this respect. The narrator does in any case take pains to point out the differences in Catherine's responses. Having learned that she must leave Northanger in the morning, Catherine finds that

> Sleep, or repose that deserved the name of sleep, was out of the question. That room, in which her disturbed imagination had tormented her on her first arrival, was again the scene of agitated spirits and unquiet slumbers. Yet how different now the source of her inquietude from what it had been then – how mournfully superior in reality and substance! Her anxiety had foundation in fact, her fears in probability; and with a mind so occupied in the contemplation of actual and natural evil, the solitude of her situation, the darkness of her chamber, the antiquity of the building were felt and considered without the smallest emotion; and though the wind was high, and

often produced strange and sudden noises throughout the house, she heard it all as she lay awake, hour after hour, without curiosity or terror (227).

These points are evidently so important that the narrator underlines them, noting that during the ride home, 'Catherine was too wretched to be fearful. The journey in itself had no terrors for her; and she began it without either dreading its length, or feeling its solitariness' (230).

Austen seems to have set herself the task of ridiculing at least two sentimental clichés and then using them seriously in the climax. She earlier mocks the particular cliché of the distressed heroine, villain and post-chaise and four, and here makes it both surprising and effective to some extent. She relies on a jolt to her reader's expectations as a means to create in him a response to a heroine's distress somewhat more fresh than usual. In the same way, she often ridicules the cliché or convention of the heroine who stands on her dignity, and then at the climax she allows Catherine to do just that with Eleanor:

the appearance of the carriage was the first thing to startle and recall them to the present moment. Catherine's colour rose at the sight of it; and the indignity with which she was treated striking at that instant on her mind with peculiar force, made her for a short time sensible only of resentment. Eleanor seemed now impelled into resolution and speech.

'You *must* write to me, Catherine,' she cried, 'you *must* let me hear from you as soon as possible. Till I know you to be safe at home, I shall not have an hour's comfort. For *one* letter, at all risks, all hazards, I must entreat. Let me have the satisfaction of knowing that you are safe at Fullerton, and have found your family well, and then, till I can ask for your correspondence as I ought to do, I will not expect more. Direct to me at Lord Longtown's, and, I must ask it, under cover to Alice.'

'No, Eleanor, if you are not allowed to receive a letter from me, I am sure I had better not write. There can be no doubt of my getting home safe' (228).

Austen is not interested, however, in using Eleanor's and Catherine's friendship to sustain or even to work up the stock sentimental conflict between pride and love. Just as Catherine is not called upon to decide whether she can stay at Northanger after the General's insult, with the result that 'neither clemency nor dignity was put to the trial' (227), so Catherine softens to Eleanor immediately: 'Eleanor only replied, ''I cannot wonder at your feelings. I will not importune you. I will trust to your own kindness of heart when I am at a distance from you." But this, with the look of sorrow accompanying it, was enough to melt Catherine's pride in a moment, and she instantly said, "Oh, Eleanor, I *will* write to you indeed"' (228–9). Austen's real interest in this conventional scene, climaxing Eleanor's and Catherine's friendship, becomes clear when it is compared with the scenes which begin their friendship. Their introduction to each other comes after the conventions of first conversations in Bath have been mocked by Henry Tilney and conversation itself has been utterly routed by Isabella Thorpe. Nevertheless, Catherine and Eleanor go 'through the first rudiments of an acquaintance, by informing themselves how well the other like Bath' (56), among other things (something Henry has specifically ridiculed); and at their second meeting, 'though in all probability not an observation was made, nor an expression used by either which had not been made and used some thousands of times before, under that roof, in every Bath season, yet the merit of their being spoken with simplicity and truth, and without personal conceit, might be something uncommon' (72). The start of their friendship shows that even the clichés and conventions of ordinary social life can enjoy some freshness if affectation is absent; similarly, the literary clichés and conventions which inform Catherine's and Eleanor's final scene together can be fresh and effective and moving when genuine, unaffected emotions replace exaggerated or self-conscious ones, in the characters and the readers both.

If Austen's design is to explore conventions in this way, its limitations must be acknowledged. She is not concerned to find more serious, genuine forms of 'distress' than conventional Gothic or sentimental ones; she confines herself very strictly to the existing conventions, and while she uses them in multiple ways, she is not attempting to manipulate her readers into any very complex or subtle, or even sustained, responses. The end follows the climax very closely, so that comic distance from Catherine's distress, from the reader's possible responses, and even from the novelist's task, is soon re-established: 'The anxiety, which in this state of their attachment must be the portion of Henry and Catherine, and of all who loved either, as to its final event, can hardly extend, I fear, to the bosom of my readers, who will see in the tell-tale compression of the pages before them, that we are all hastening together to perfect felicity' (250).

5. MANIPULATION OF GOTHIC CONVENTION

Northanger Abbey turns on manipulating and teasing the reader's judgments of what will happen – will events be like life? like literature? – rather than his judgments of or feelings for characters. While this concern imposes a severe limitation on the novel, Austen does manage to show, in her treatment of Gothic convention, the power that this straightforward concern with plot, with what will happen, can have over a reader. For this reason, her treatment of the Gothic conventions is more skilful and more interesting than her treatment of the convention of distress, though her aims and techniques are nearly identical. In both cases, she starts by debunking the conventions, and then she exploits them. Her ridicule of Gothic conventions is, however, more thorough and is more immediately followed by her attempt to produce with them the very curiosity, tension, suspense and apprehension they aim at, which Henry Tilney has just mocked and Catherine has just repudiated.

Henry's mockery of Gothic conventions takes the form of a very memorable, sustained parody in which he imagines several Gothic adventures for Catherine at the Abbey. The parody has many functions, the first of which is sheer comedy. Austen takes the opportunity to revel in the clichés of Gothic fiction, not simply its stock situations and stock props, though Henry conflates these brilliantly, but also its stock descriptive phrases. In his opening paragraph, Henry assembles the hackneyed adjectives of Gothic description: the 'dimly lighted' hall, the 'expiring embers' of a fire, the 'ancient housekeeper', 'gloomy passages', and 'gloomy chamber – too lofty and extensive', the 'feeble rays of a single lamp', the 'walls hung with tapestry exhibiting figures as large as life, and the bed, of dark green stuff or purple velvet, presenting even a funereal appearance' (158). These clichés are relentlessly pursued throughout his narration, reaching a kind of climax in the 'violent storm' he evokes for the adventure, complete with 'Peals of thunder' which 'roll round the neighbouring mountains' and 'shake the edifice to its foundation', and with 'frightful gusts of wind' which will allow Catherine to see 'one part of the hanging more violently agitated than the rest' (159). But although Gothic machinery is concentrated here, it actually spreads itself throughout, from the 'broken lute' and 'ponderous chest which no efforts can open' to the lamp which 'suddenly expires in the socket' producing 'total darkness' – and the end of Henry's story.

More interesting comedy results from the clichés which Henry uses for emotional responses: at first, 'Will not your mind misgive you,' and 'Will not your heart sink within you?' and later, 'fainting spirits', 'increased

alarm', '*unconquerable* horror', 'irresistible presentiment'. These responses, so typical of Gothic heroines, are cleverly juxtaposed with
Catherine's immediate responses to the narrative, suggesting the stock
but strong responses of the reader of Gothic fiction: disbelief coupled
with imaginative belief. 'Oh! Mr Tilney, how frightful! – This is just like
a book! – But it cannot really happen to me. I am sure your housekeeper
is not really Dorothy. – Well, what then?' (159). Austen's effects here are
especially complex. She is calling attention to the comic incongruity
between the average reader's immediate involvement with the plot, his
eagerness for what will happen next, and his distance from it, his
enjoyment of what the narrator calls 'the luxury of a raised, restless, and
frightened imagination' (51). Although Austen laughs at this combination of distance and involvement, and particularly at involvement
with conventions so hackneyed, she will insist, in her next chapters, on
her reader's responding in precisely the same way.

Henry's parody foreshadows, in a crude way, just how Austen will
bring off this feat, and this constitutes its second function. His narrative is
punctuated by some especially heavy sarcasms at the expense of Gothic
convention which are aimed at the reader and, naturally, wholly
unperceived by Catherine: 'To raise your spirits, moreover, [the house-
keeper] gives you reason to suppose that the part of the abbey you inhabit is undoubtedly haunted'; 'After surmounting your *unconquerable*
horror of the bed'; 'which door being only secured by massy bars and a
padlock, you will, after a few efforts, succeed in opening'; and above all,
'you will proceed into this small vaulted room, and through this into
several others, without perceiving any thing very remarkable in either. In
one perhaps there may be a dagger, in another a few drops of blood, and
in a third the remains of some instrument of torture; but there [is]
nothing in all this out of the common way ...' (160). These sarcasms,
which merely underline Catherine's imperception as well as some of the
most flagrant Gothic absurdities, interrupt more effective parody, and
would be simply another gauge of the novel's youthfulness, if they did
not indicate something else: the extreme care with which Austen has
designed her Gothic parody. Henry's rather abrupt alternations between
imitative parody and sarcasm prefigure the far more subtle modulations
between imitation and irony in the narration of Catherine's adventures at
Northanger; these allow Austen to play endless tricks on her readers.
Henry's crudeness, however, lulls the reader into expecting (and
sometimes, as many critcs attest, into perceiving) only very crude parody.

A final use for Henry's narrative is to influence Catherine's adventures:
many parallels exist between them, and 'Henry's words, his des-

cription of the ebony cabinet which was to escape her observation at first' (168) explicitly spur Catherine to her second adventure, and comfort her after it: 'Heaven forbid that Henry Tilney should ever know her folly! And it was in a great measure his own doing, for had not the cabinet appeared so exactly to agree with his description of her adventures, she should never have felt the smallest curiosity about it' (173). The parody does serve to make Catherine's adventures somewhat more credible psychologically, but more important, it underlines the power of the very conventions and devices it ridicules. Catherine assures Henry and herself that 'her attention had been fixed [to his narrative] without the smallest apprehension of really meeting with what he related. "Miss Tilney, she was sure, would never put her into such a chamber as he had described! – She was not at all afraid" ' (160), and then promptly sees herself in just such a chamber. Similarly, the reader, taught by Henry to expect only deflation for the Gothic, finds himself caught up in it despite all the mockery he has encountered and enjoyed.

Catherine's brief first adventure, the 'mysterious chest', reinforces and extends for her and for the reader the effects of Henry's parody. When her 'astonished eyes' behold the 'white cotton counterpane, properly folded, reposing at one end of the chest in undisputed possession' (164), the reader is lulled once more with fairly simple parody. But even here, something slightly more intricate is happening. The pattern for future adventures is set and extends the one used to deflate sentimental conventions. Austen begins by firmly establishing a comic tone. She then introduces a somewhat more serious interlude in which Gothic devices and effects are carefully imitated. Finally she returns to comedy. Thus Catherine's first thoughts 'when her eye suddenly fell on a large high chest, standing back in a deep recess on one side of the fire-place' are purely comic. 'This is strange indeed! I did not expect such a sight as this! – An immense heavy chest! – What can it hold? – Why should it be placed here? – Pushed back too, as if meant to be out of sight! – I will look into it – cost me what it may, I will look into it – and directly too – by day-light. If I stay till evening my candle may go out' (163). As the narration continues, however, distinctly Radcliffean description begins to prevail, though here with subtle modulations between imitation ('curiously inlaid', 'tarnished from age') and burlesque ('strange violence', 'mysterious cypher', 'strange events') which establish ironic distance, indicating that the feelings evoked are to be laughed at and that Catherine's imagination is 'raised':

She advanced and examined it closely: it was of cedar, curiously inlaid with some darker wood, and raised, about a foot from the ground, on a carved stand of the same. The lock was silver, though tarnished from age; at each end were the imperfect remains of handles also of silver, broken perhaps prematurely by some strange violence; and, on the centre of the lid, was a mysterious cypher, in the same metal. Catherine bent over it intently, but without being able to distinguish any thing with certainty. She could not, in whatever direction she took it, believe the last letter to be a *T*; and yet that it should be any thing else in that house was a circumstance to raise no common degree of astonishment. If not originally their's, by what strange events could it have fallen into the Tilney family? (163–4).

The extensive visual detail, so unusual in Austen's prose and in fact so consciously excluded from it, deliberately mirrors (especially in common with fearful conjectures) one of Mrs Radcliffe's chief devices, and the next passage duplicates another, producing a climax: 'Her fearful curiosity was every moment growing greater; and seizing, with trembling hands, the hasp of the lock, she resolved at all hazards to satisfy herself at least as to its contents. With difficulty, for something seemed to resist her efforts, she raised the lid a few inches; but at that moment a sudden knocking at the door of the room made her, starting, quit her hold, and the lid closed with alarming violence' (164). The trite interruption, and the heightened description which precedes it, actually have some effect on the reader: some apprehension and expectation are created simply because Austen uses these clichés seriously and allows Catherine to register fear. These responses are created only to be dispelled, of course, for immediately after the interruption the clearest possible comic irony reappears. Catherine examines the 'object so well calculated to interest and alarm' half dressed, 'having slipped one arm into her gown'; and this anti-heroic posture emphasizes the absurdity of her resolution: 'so desperate should be the exertion of her strength, that, unless secured by supernatural means, the lid in one moment should be thrown back. With this spirit she sprang forward, and her confidence did not deceive her' (164). The comic anticlimax follows: she discovers the counterpane.

The second adventure, of the 'mysterious manuscript,' follows hard upon the first but is treated more seriously. Its middle section, directly imitating Gothic devices, is more sustained and more effective, and also ends a chapter, so that comedy is not securely regained until the next chapter. This section, too, is highly complex, for within it Austen modulates between close imitation of Gothic conventions and several methods of distancing the reader from them and the expectations they create. Yet so thoroughly does her imitation exploit the conventions that her Gothic effects are actually more powerful than those of her model, Ann Radcliffe, even in her more celebrated passages. Austen's interest in and improvement upon Radcliffe's Gothic effects are, however, more easily claimed than demonstrated. One major difficulty lies in isolating passages from Radcliffe's works which can be set fairly against Austen's imitation. All Radcliffe's effects suffer slightly when her scenes are separated from their contexts. Furthermore, no direct evidence exists for Austen's preferences, if any, among her scenes or her works; we do not even know at which 'most interesting part' of *The Mysteries of Udolpho* Henry Tilney refused to interrupt his reading for five minutes (107).

Still, Austen does imply a kind of fascination with the scenes (usually climactic) in which the Radcliffe heroine discovers something shocking or mysterious, for she imitates these almost exclusively. Unfortunately, her imitation is seldom direct; no clear models for Catherine's adventures at Northanger can be found in Radcliffe. The adventures imagined for Catherine by Henry, however, do have analogues, and Chapman reprints in the appendices to his edition of *Northanger Abbey* and *Persuasion* a passage from *The Romance of the Forest* (1791) 'which bears a closer resemblance to the adventures of Catherine Morland . . . than anything to be found in *Udolpho* itself' (*P*, p. 285). Adeline's discovery of a mysterious manuscript in *The Romance of the Forest* is at two removes from Catherine's discovery of the washing-bills: Catherine's adventures partly imitate events in Henry's parody, and these events burlesque several elements in Adeline's discovery scene. Despite this indirection, some measure of the differences between Austen's effects and Radcliffe's can be approximated by comparing the climactic moments of the scenes: the heroines' discoveries and immediate responses. In *The Romance of the Forest*, Adeline discovers 'an old dagger': 'with a trembling hand she took it up, and upon a closer view perceived, that it was spotted and stained with rust. Shocked and surprised, she looked round the room for some object that might confirm or destroy the dreadful suspicion which now rushed upon her mind.'[10] 'Shocked and surprised,' though anticlimactic, is less so than the 'curiosity and terror' and 'the solemnity of Adeline's feelings' which accompany her discovery of the manuscript itself. Having disturbed a 'confused heap' of old, broken furniture, so that it falls toward her,

> Adeline started aside and saved herself, and when the noise it made had ceased, she heard a small rustling sound, and as she was about to leave the chamber, saw something falling gently among the lumber.

It was a small roll of paper, tied with a string, and covered with dust. Adeline took it up, and on opening it perceived an handwriting. She attempted to read it, but the part of the manuscript she looked at was so much obliterated, that she found this difficult, though what few words were legible impressed her with curiosity and terror, and induced her to return with it immediately to her chamber.

Having reached her own room, she fastened the private door, and let the arras fall over it as before. It was now midnight. The stillness of the hour, interrupted only at intervals by the hollow sighings of the blast, heightened the solemnity of Adeline's feelings.[11]

The parallel passage in *Northanger Abbey* much more effectively elicits tension and suspense, again, largely because Austen's mastery of descriptive detail and sentence flow, and her power to create intimacy with her heroine, are immeasurably greater than Radcliffe's. At the same time, however, Austen demands that intimacy with Catherine's fears alternate with distance from them. She uses Catherine's prosaic and incongruous commentary ('she had "never from the first had the smallest idea of finding any thing"'), her even more incongruous actions (she 'sought some suspension of agony by creeping far underneath the [bed] clothes'), and, above all, a heightened, exaggerated rhetoric ('Darkness impenetrable and immovable') to qualify the suspense she raises simply by using Gothic conventions: a discovery, an interruption, darkness, isolation, and fearfulness.

The place in the middle alone remained now unexplored; and though she had 'never from the first had the smallest idea of finding any thing in any part of the cabinet, and was not in the least disappointed at her ill success thus far, it would be foolish not to examine it thoroughly while she was about it.' It was some time however before she could unfasten the door, the same difficulty occurring in the management of this inner lock as of the outer; but at length it did open; and not vain, as hitherto, was her search; her quick eyes directly fell on a roll of paper pushed back into the further part of the cavity, apparently for concealment, and her feelings at that moment were indescribable. Her heart fluttered, her knees trembled, and her cheeks grew pale. She seized, with an unsteady hand, the precious manuscript, for half a glance sufficed to ascertain written characters; and while she acknowledged with awful sensations this striking exemplification of what Henry had foretold, resolved instantly to peruse every line before she attempted to rest.

The dimness of the light her candle emitted made her turn to it with alarm; but there was no danger of its sudden extinction, it had yet some hours to burn; and that she might not have any greater difficulty in distinguishing the writing than what its ancient date might occasion, she hastily snuffed it. Alas! it was snuffed and extinguished in one. A lamp could not have expired with more awful effect. Catherine, for a few moments, was motionless with horror. It was done completely; not a remnant of light in the wick could give hope to the rekindling breath. Darkness impenetrable and immovable filled the room. A violent gust of wind, rising with sudden fury, added fresh horror to the moment. Catherine trembled from head to foot. In the pause which succeeded, a sound like receding footsteps and the closing of a distant door struck on her affrighted ear. Human nature could support no more. A cold sweat stood on her forehead, the manuscript fell from her hand, and groping her way to the bed, she jumped hastily in, and sought some suspension of agony by creeping far underneath the clothes (169–70).

The rest of the passage is even more complex. Examined apart, each sentence is full of irony at Catherine's hackneyed fears and conjectures or at the language which conveys them ('fraught with awful intelligence', 'startled ear', 'Hollow murmurs', 'blood was chilled'). The conclusion, Catherine's falling asleep, nicely undercuts her expectation that 'repose must be absolutely impossible'. Yet on the whole the passage makes the reader feel for and with Catherine rather than distant from her. Austen's writing has seldom been more perfectly controlled:

To close her eyes in sleep that night, she felt must be entirely out of the question. With a curiosity so justly awakened, and feelings in every way so agitated, repose must be absolutely impossible. The storm too abroad so dreadful! – She had not been used to feel alarm from wind, but now every blast seemed fraught with awful intelligence. The manuscript so wonderfully found, so wonderfully accomplishing the morning's prediction, how was it to be accounted for? – What could it contain? – to whom could it relate? – by what means could it have been so long concealed? – and how singularly strange that it should fall to her lot to discover it! Till she had made herself mistress of its contents, however, she could have neither repose nor comfort; and with the sun's first rays she was determined to peruse it. But many were the tedious hours which must yet intervene. She shuddered, tossed about in her bed, and envied every quiet sleeper. The storm still raged, and various were the noises, more terrific even than the wind, which struck at intervals on her startled ear. The very curtains of her bed seemed at one moment in motion, and at another the lock of her door was agitated, as if by the attempt of somebody to enter. Hollow murmurs seemed to creep along the gallery, and more than once her blood was chilled by the sound of distant moans. Hour after hour passed away, and the wearied Catherine had heard three proclaimed by all the clocks in the house, before the tempest subsided, or she unknowingly fell fast asleep (170–1).

The marvellous decrescendo and closure of the last phrase perfectly effects a return to prose from the previous sentence, which has climaxed the heightened rhetoric of the passage with long vowel sounds and the regular rhythms of poetry.

Such writing is not mere burlesque. In one of her letters, Austen describes Eaton Stannard Barrett's *The Heroine, or Adventures of a Fair Romance Reader* (1813) as 'a delightful burlesque, particularly on the Radcliffe style' (*L*, p. 377), and this definition is adequate, although Austen's delight may surprise anyone who has read *The Heroine*. Barrett's treatment of the Radcliffe heroine's discovery scene suggests what Austen might have done if her interest lay simply in burlesque, and shows how much less effective the Gothic sections in *Northanger Abbey* would have been in that case:

With a trembling hand I opened a door, and found myself in a circular chamber, which was furnished with musical instruments. Intending to run my fingers over the keys of a piano, I walked towards it, till a low rustling made me pause. But what was my confusion, when I heard the mysterious machine on sudden begin to sound; not loudly, but (more terrible still!) with a hurried murmur; as if all its chords were agitated at once, by the hand of some invisible spirit.

I did not faint, I did not shriek; but I stood transfixed to the spot. The music ceased. I recovered courage, and advanced. The music began again; and again I paused.

What! should I shrink from lifting the simple lid of a mere piano? What! should I resign the palm of hardihood to Emily, who drew aside the black veil, and discovered the terrific wax-doll underneath it?

Emulation, enthusiasm, curiosity prompted me, and I rushed undaunted to the piano. Louder and more rapid grew the notes – my desperate hand raised the cover, and beneath it, I beheld a sight to me the most hideous and fearful upon earth, – a mouse!

I shrieked, and dropped the candle, which was instantly extinguished. The mouse ran by my feet; I flew towards the door, but
missed it, and fell against a table; nor till after I had made a most
alarming clamour, could I get out of the room.[12]

Barrett can arrange an anticlimax to mock the absurdity of Gothic
devices, but he shows no feeling for the emotional powers of Gothic
fiction. Austen evidently has such a feeling. At any rate, she can combine
imitation with mockery or burlesque so as to obtain a Gothic climax
rather more powerful than any of Mrs Radcliffe's and so as to mock it at
the same time.

The final Gothic adventure in *Northanger Abbey* is the lengthiest and
most discussed: Catherine's reading of General Tilney as a Radcliffean
villain. The same pattern, comic development succeeded by a Gothic
climax and a comic anticlimax, is extended to include several successive,
increasingly tense climaxes, which occur whenever Catherine's
explorations of Mrs Tilney's room are interrupted. She and Eleanor
Tilney are first prevented from approaching the room when the General
calls Eleanor 'hastily, and, as Catherine thought, rather angrily back,
demanding whither she were going?' (185). The second interruption is
more alarming, and in fact perfectly imitates Radcliffe: 'Again [Eleanor]
passed through the folding-doors, again her hand was upon the important
lock, and Catherine, hardly able to breathe, was turning to close the
former with fearful caution, when the figure, the dreaded figure of the
General himself at the further end of the gallery, stood before her! The
name of "Eleanor" at the same moment, in his loudest tone, resounded
through the building, giving to his daughter the first intimation of his
presence, and to Catherine terror upon terror' (191–2). Catherine reaches
the room alone in the final incident, and though her feelings when she
discovers merely a handsome, modern apartment are 'worked', she
quickly resumes her suspicions, and two separate climaxes follow at once:
a purely Gothic and surprisingly effective one, in which she is interrupted
by the noise of someone's approach and she listens 'With a feeling of
terror not very definable' to footsteps coming up the stairs (194). Henry
Tilney appears, both are surprised, and the incident results in the final
climax to the Gothic section: Henry's oft-quoted rebuke to Catherine's
suspicions.

The suspense and apprehension created by these incidents depend partly
on the simply device of interruption, but more on the treatment of
General Tilney's character. As Marvin Mudrick points out, the General
arouses the reader's 'interest in his nature and his motives'. For Mudrick,

however, 'the suspense aroused by our uncertainty about him' provides 'realistic scaffolding' for the Gothic episode which is in turn fatally undermined by the General's inconsistencies as a character.[13] But realism is hardly Austen's object. She intends the General to be not only mysterious, a quality Mudrick concedes, but also menacing, to the reader as well as to Catherine, although the reader never shares Catherine's delusion that he imprisoned or murdered his wife, and although the reader is also not asked to exercise his moral perceptiveness in detecting the General's villainy. His prosaic faults, gluttony, avarice and egoism, are quite openly conveyed to the reader over Catherine's head in much the same way as are Isabella Thorpe's. The joke lies in Catherine's imperception.

Earlier, however, the groundwork is laid for the General's more sinister qualities. At Bath, his children's constraint around him is clearly established, and both Catherine and the reader are 'puzzled' that she finds it 'a release to get away from him' despite his civilities and compliments to her (129). At Northanger, the General's presence becomes more and more oppressive. His children's discomfort increases, as do his fulsome compliments, and more conventional hints of Gothic villainy multiply: his explosions of bad temper, his domestic tyranny and Eleanor's evident melancholy are added to the interruptions of Catherine's explorations. Austen intersperses this direct reliance on Gothic conventions with ironic treatment. Like the 'mysterious chest' and the 'mysterious manuscript', the 'mysterious tyrant' is debunked as well as exploited. Thus Catherine reflects, 'This lengthened absence, these solitary rambles, did not speak a mind at ease, or a conscience void of reproach' (182), and at last discerns 'the air and attitude of a Montoni!' in the General's 'slowly pacing the drawing-room for an hour together in silent thoughtfulness, with downcast eyes and contracted brow' (187). These broadly comic passages distance the reader from the discomfort and even threat conveyed by the General's very real anger and by his mistreatment of Eleanor. A particularly effective instance of the former occurs just after Catherine's adventure with the chest, so that a genuine alarm (however transient) succeeds the false one: 'Miss Tilney gently hinted her fear of being late; and in half a minute they ran down stairs together, in an alarm not wholly unfounded, for General Tilney was pacing the drawing-room, his watch in his hand, and having, on the very instant of their entering, pulled the bell with violence, ordered "Dinner to be on table *directly*!" ' (165).

The General's peremptoriness and injustice to Eleanor are even more unpleasant. Austen makes Eleanor Tilney into something of a Gothic heroine at Northanger. Like conventional Radcliffe heroines, Eleanor is subject to a tyrant's whims and sometimes is melancholy, yet she supports her lot with fortitude and (here departing from the conventions) with cheerfulness. Austen is careful to imply rather than proclaim that Eleanor is a Gothic heroine, for the corollary, that the General is truly a Gothic villain, would not serve her purposes. She wants the General to be felt by the reader as menacing and repellant, but only Catherine is to label him a Montoni. The reader is meant to be puzzled and curious about the General's behaviour, and is not meant to explain it to himself by deducing the General's mistaken notion of Catherine's wealth. Austen provides dues to his motives, but these are not emphasized, unlike her indications of Wickham's or Frank Churchill's characters in the later novels. Austen is thus free to shock the reader with the General's expulsion of Catherine and to present her final joke on readers and novels alike: in a dénouement equally typical of Gothic and sentimental novels, Eleanor is revealed as a heroine indeed, in love with and at last united to a poor suitor who unexpectedly acquires wealth and a title, and hence a wife. This circumstance softens the General, and he sanctions Henry's marriage to Catherine at last.

In *Northanger Abbey*, Jane Austen both exploits and mocks the conventions of the contemporary novel. She delights in her power to debunk these conventions and then make them work. She is not principally concerned to defend or to condemn contemporary fiction. Instead, she examines the conventions of contemporary fiction in order to expose and delight in both their absurdity and their power to engross the imagination and to create a response. She is not yet interested in harnessing these conventions to a higher use or to more complex designs. Or perhaps more correctly, she is not yet mature enough as an artist to use conventions without self-consciousness, without calling attention to their presence. At the same time, this interest in convention offers her a good start as a novelist – a far more promising one, in general, than that exclusive interest in oneself which produces so many autobiographical first novels. Those writers whose early works show, like Austen's, a playful treatment of convention, an attraction to artifice, and an amused preoccupation with the relation between life and literature, are among the greatest; these concerns are visible in the early work of Chaucer (*The Book of the Duchess*) and Shakespeare (*Love's Labour's Lost*). Austen can be said, like them, to absorb convention into her comedy and at last to transcend it.

This process is traceable also in the work of certain other novelists, whose development, while distinct from Austen's, is comparable to hers. Henry James in *Watch and Ward* (published serially 1871; separately 1878), is interested in how much the relations and perceptions of life are influenced by the images and plots of literature. The characters in *Watch and Ward* have literary preconceptions and expectations; their imaginations are consciously bookish even when they see themselves as anti-heroic. The novel, like *Northanger Abbey*, ends like a novel and says so; all the conventions are self-consciously exploited. E. M. Forster is as fond of literary jokes as Austen: witness the incident in *A Room With a View* (1908) in which Miss Lavish makes a cheap novel out of Lucy Honeychurch's adventure in the Piazza. More important, although Forster is always, unlike Austen, more interested in exploring the influence and limits of social rather than literary convention, he began, like her, by writing novels which were inspired by those of his contemporaries.[14]

Novelists who openly display literary convention and incorporate literary allusion in their work easily obtain one advantage: they force their readers to be conscious of the process of reading. This demand can be intrusive and tedious in tactless, pompous or careless hands. Yet James, Forster and Austen avoid exasperating their readers and can instead use this technique to complicate their readers' responses with reminders of alternate representations of life, alternate appeals to the emotions and imagination, alternate sets of expectations.

This technique can have, equally, the great disadvantage of being rather too brilliant and calculated. In *Northanger Abbey*, manipulation of literary convention becomes a *tour de force* which takes the place of everything the next two novels exhibit: fuller relations between the characters; more complex exploration of the themes; and a didactic intention which entails subtle and profound manipulation of judgment and sympathy, responses to literature (and to life) which are far more complex and more significant than the suspense and distress considered in *Northanger Abbey*. The more substantial themes and techniques and the more serious didactic intentions of *Sense and Sensibility* and *Pride and Prejudice* do not, however, preclude examination and ridicule of literary convention. In *Sense and Sensibility*, for example, the effect of literary conventions and expectations upon emotion and conduct is explored within the character of Marianne Dashwood; the theme is assimilated to character. *Northanger Abbey*, then, is not central to Jane Austen's concerns or achievements; *Sense and Sensibilty* is.

2 *Sense and Sensibility*

In *Sense and Sensibility* (1811), Austen's most characteristic themes are recognizable as they are not in *Northanger Abbey*, and she begins to develop methods to embody them which foreshadow the techniques of her later fiction. *Sense and Sensibility* is, as a result, far more interesting and mature than *Northanger Abbey*, although both are still 'bookish' works, calling attention to the literary conventions which they exploit and expose. In *Northanger Abbey*, Austen seems to be frustrating, jolting and manipulating her readers' conventional expectations and responses largely for fun. Judging and responding to the characters is never problematic, for either they are as transparent as Isabella Thorpe, Captain Tilney and Catherine herself, or speculation about them is confined to plot: will General Tilney's actions be like life or like literature? In *Sense and Sensibility* and the later novels, however, Austen elicits and manipulates the responses of judgment and sympathy, with a moral intention: to exercise, to develop and finally to educate these responses in her readers. As literary responses, judgment and sympathy differ from suspense and distress principally by engaging and implicating a reader more formidably: exercising judgement and sympathy challenges and tests a reader's perceptions, emotions, intelligence and moral sense. To elicit these requires a more complex world and subtler discriminations than those of *Northanger Abbey*, and in *Sense and Sensibility* Austen learns to obtain these effects almost entirely by constructing elaborate parallels and contrasts between characters. She never abandons these concerns or these techniques, although she subsequently complicates and refines them. *Sense and Sensibility* thus resembles Austen's later work in significant ways, and is at the same time simpler and more accessible, offering a helpful approach to the later novels and providing a standard against which her achievement in them can be measured.

1. CRITICAL VIEWS OF *SENSE AND SENSIBILITY*

Perhaps because prefigurations of the later fiction are so evident and, by comparison, so disappointing, critics have appreciated *Sense and Sensibility*

39

least of all Austen's novels, and Elinor Dashwood least of the heroines; even Fanny Price and *Mansfield Park* have received better treatment. Judgments that the novel is 'extremely rigid'[1] and that Elinor is 'priggish and self-righteous'[2] have been widely accepted. These ideas seem to derive from a critical error and a critical bias respectively. The error is made by critics who interpret 'sensibility' as synonymous with feeling and with qualities even more precious to moderns: openness and spontaneity. These critics overlook Austen's careful definition, that sensibility is not merely a capacity to feel but a set of attitudes toward feeling, which is 'valued and cherished', sought and indulged (7). To ignore this distinction is to conclude, despite insistent and continual contradiction by the text, that in proportion as Elinor lacks 'sensibility', she lacks feeling, a conclusion which renders her odious. Mudrick's especially perverse reading is apposite: 'Elinor rebukes Marianne by implying that in her still disappointed love for Edward she is as unhappy as Marianne but has kept silent because of "what I owed to my dearest friends" . . . (an implication for which one would be hard put to find evidence in the novel, where Elinor seems amorously moved only by Willoughby'.[3] It is impossible to decide what is more exasperating in these remarks: the view of Elinor as having strong feelings only for Willoughby, or the twofold denial of Elinor's unhappiness and of her concern to spare her mother and sister the sight of it, an unhappiness and a concern Austen repeatedly emphasizes. For Mudrick, Austen is guilty of a surrender to 'social convention'[4] by weighting the novel in favour of Elinor's propriety and restraint. Such objections anticipate those sometimes made to *Mansfield Park*, whose affinity to *Sense and Sensibility* is often felt, and which has been until recently similarly misunderstood and undervalued.

The error of denying, distorting or minimizing Elinor's feelings has a corollary in the error of critics who detect in any demonstration of feeling on Elinor's part a movement of 'sense' toward 'sensibility', a movement toward an intended reconciliation of the two. Observing that Elinor is 'stirred' by her 'suitor' Edward Ferrars, Wright decides that, 'already the sensibility of Elinor has been awakened. The elder sister may still be able to give counsels of sense; but she has already tasted the values of sensibility.'[5] At no time, however, is Austen concerned to present 'the values of sensibility'. On the contrary, she demonstrates that the doctrines of sensibility betray real feeling, and result in behaviour that is totally unfeeling. One of Austen's major interests in the novel is to define feeling and sensitive behaviour, and she shows that it includes a capacity to estimate and appreciate others' feelings along with a willingness to act so as to consider those feelings as much as possible. This behaviour is

what Elinor exhibits and Marianne violates throughout the novel. It is
Marianne who must learn to behave feelingly, not Elinor. Elinor's
behaviour and the feelings which prompt it are, from the beginning,
considerate and right.

This view would make *Sense and Sensibility* all the more unpalatable to
those critics who dislike it because of their bias in favour of irony. Their
tendency is not merely to place a high value on irony, but to expect and
even to demand it in every book by Austen. Because Marianne is treated
ironically, and because her 'sensibility' is shown to need correction, they
feel that Elinor's 'sense' should be exposed as deficient, or as equally in
need of correction and modification. These readers' expectation and desire
for such a countermovement is so great that, naturally enough, some have
come to detect it in the design of the novel. Such criticism assumes that
some middle ground is reached between Elinor and Marianne, which
involves the assumption that Elinor needs correction, usually that she is in
some way unfeeling at first and learns in the course of the action to taste
'the values of sensibility'. The irony with which her situation *is* treated is
generally overlooked, even by those critics who view her character
favourably. This irony is, however, at the centre of the novel and forms
its emotional and thematic core. For Elinor's continual exertions to
control her feelings, to appear cheerful when she is unhappy and to be
considerate of her mother and sister in order that they be 'spared much
solicitude on her account' (104), lead Mrs Dashwood and Marianne to
assume – along with some of the critics – that in fact she has no feelings.
This situation, as it is presented and developed by the action, embodies
two central ironic perceptions. First, consideration for others' feelings
permits others to be inconsiderate of one's own. Secondly, excess of
sensibility (in Marianne and Mrs Dashwood) becomes insensibility –
insensitivity to and misjudgment of others' feelings.[6] As a result, Elinor is
given credit neither for having feelings nor for commanding them.
Austen insists, however, that the consideration and self-command Elinor
shows are not any the less required of her for being invariably
misunderstood and unrewarded. They remain, absolutely and
imperatively, an obligation.

All these points are made quietly, and with a complete absence of self-
pity and even self-righteousness. No plaintive or bitter note is sounded.
Yet what is presented is a harsh and uncompromising vision of the
emotional tensions and costs of moral behaviour. In *Sense and Sensibility*,
'feeling' for others, a quality endowed with both an emotional and a
moral dimension, is an obligation which, however necessary it is to the
decencies of social life, may easily go unnoticed and unappreciated by

those who benefit from it. Moreover, it is often painful in itself, comprising the pain of suppressing one's own feelings and the pain of participating in others' sufferings. Such is the clarity, complexity and austerity of moral vision and emotional awareness that Austen masters in her first published work. It is an impressive achievement, and one which highlights the subtler and more mellow visions of the later novels.

This estimate of *Sense and Sensibility* is rare partly because the novel suffers from the highly visible and even obtrusive technique of contrast chosen to embody its themes. The reader's attention is so overwhelmed by the complicated, clever and insistent symmetries, doublings, parallels, contrasts and comparisons among characters and actions and even chapters which form the surface of *Sense and Sensibility* that he may be driven to conclude that nothing lies beneath and to apply a critical cliché: the greater the technical skill, the greater the likelihood that it is an end in itself, submerging emotional content and thereby rendering an intricate structure lifeless or mechanical. Like all clichés, this one contains a seductive portion of truth, and critics who approach *Sense and Sensibility* through its connections to the characters, motifs or debates commonly found in eighteenth-century novels are especially tempted by it, probably because their work has entailed reading so many lifeless and mechanical eighteenth-century novels constructed upon similar principles of contrast. Distinctions blur under such strains. Whether Austen's novel succumbs to a 'tyranny of antithesis'[7] or whether it succeeds finally in constructing contrasts and antitheses which give expression and life to her perceptions of moral and emotional experience cannot be determined merely by close examination of its structure; but an answer must begin there.

2. THE STRUCTURE OF *SENSE AND SENSIBILITY*

The first chapter sets up almost all the contrasts which will be refined and worked out through the novel, and the chapters which immediately follow extend them, partly by dramatization. Self-interest (or selfishness) and coldness are carefully contrasted with warmth and generosity. Mrs Dashwood, her husband and her children have lived with and attended their uncle, the owner of Norland, 'not merely from interest, but from goodness of heart' (3). The 'rather cold hearted, and rather selfish' disposition of John Dashwood opposes 'the strong feelings of the rest of the family' (5) and beyond him lies his wife: 'Mrs John Dashwood was a strong caricature of himself; – more narrow-minded and selfish' (5).

Similarly, the impulsiveness and 'romantic' generosity (6) of Mrs
Dashwood is, on the one hand, set against Mrs John Dashwood's
rudeness in arriving at Norland immediately after the funeral, 'shewing
them with how little attention to the comfort of other people she could
act when occasion required it' (6), and, on the other, against John
Dashwood's careful calculation that he can give his sisters three thousand
pounds in fulfilment of his promise to his father, because his own greatly
increased fortune at his father's death 'warmed his heart and made him
feel capable of generosity' (5).

Once these broad contrasts are outlined, Austen is free to initiate
subtler ones among the characters whose essential goodness has been
established. Having pointed to the unfeeling or calculated behaviour of
selfish people, Austen hints at a more interesting theme, the unfeeling or
thoughtless behaviour good people can be guilty of. Mrs Dashwood, for
instance, 'would have quitted the house for ever' in disgust with
Mrs John Dashwood's rudeness and would thus have been guilty of
parallel, though not comparable, impoliteness, but she is brought 'to
reflect on the propriety of going' (6). This reflection introduces another
important theme, that propriety or politeness remains imperative, however rude one's associates. The theme of unrewarded but nonetheless
obligatory consideration for others is sounded in harsher tones at the start
of the chapter. The former owner of Norland ties up his property for the
benefit of his four-year-old great-nephew, because the child's 'attractions
. . . outweigh all the value of all attention which, for years, he had
received from his niece and her daughters' (4).

The most significant contrasts defined by the first chapter, those
between Elinor and Marianne and between 'sense' and 'sensibility', are
reserved for its last four paragraphs:

Elinor, this eldest daughter whose advice was so effectual, possessed
a strength of understanding, and coolness of judgment, which qualified
her, though only nineteen, to be the counsellor of her mother, and
enabled her frequently to counteract, to the advantage of them all, that
eagerness of mind in Mrs Dashwood which must generally have led to
imprudence. She had an excellent heart; – her disposition was
affectionate, and her feelings were strong; but she knew how to govern
them: it was a knowledge which her mother had yet to learn, and
which one of her sisters had resolved never to be taught.

Marianne's abilities were, in many respects, quite equal to Elinor's.
She was sensible and clever; but eager in every thing; her sorrows, her
joys, could have no moderation. She was generous, amiable, in-

teresting: she was every thing but prudent. The resemblance between her and her mother was strikingly great.

Elinor saw, with concern, the excess of her sister's sensibility; but by Mrs Dashwood it was valued and cherished. They encouraged each other now in the violence of their affliction. The agony of grief which overpowered them at first, was voluntarily renewed, was sought for, was created again and again. They gave themselves up wholly to their sorrow, seeking increase of wretchedness in every reflection that could afford it, and resolved against ever admitting consolation in future. Elinor, too, was deeply afflicted; but still she could struggle, she could exert herself. She could consult with her brother, could receive her sister-in-law on her arrival, and treat her with proper attention; and could strive to rouse her mother to similar exertion, and encourage her to similar forbearance.

Margaret, the other sister, was a good-humoured well-disposed girl; but as she had already imbibed a good deal of Marianne's romance, without having much of her sense, she did not, at thirteen, bid fair to equal her sisters at a more advanced period of life (6–7).

While this passage does contain antithetical terms, 'sense' and 'sensibility' are not among them. 'Sensibility', the more easily defined of the two, appears only once, in conjunction with 'excess', and what constitutes that excess is specified: emotions are 'valued and cherished' for their own sake and therefore every attempt is made to sustain and increase them. A distinction is explicitly made between emotions which necessarily but temporarily overwhelm people of strong feelings, and emotions which are deliberately sought and indulged. As Marianne embodies it, and as the eighteenth century conceived it, sensibility is not merely emotion itself but a set of attitudes toward emotion forming a theory of its nature and value. This theory is throughout the novel placed in opposition to Elinor's. Unlike Marianne, Elinor sees no special virtue in emotional intensity but values instead kindness, consideration and courtesy, along with the ability to practice these in spite of what one is feeling; thus she 'could struggle' to receive her sister-in-law 'with proper attention'. Implicit in both Elinor's and Marianne's attitudes is the recognition that very strong feeling caused by a sudden event is temporary. Elinor accepts this transience as a condition of life which makes it easier to live, while Marianne combats it as a condition which threatens her notion of what life should be.

Such oppositions form the contrast and conflict between Elinor and Marianne, but it is important to recognize their underlying similarities.

In both, behaviour proceeds from principles or judgments, that is, from rational notions about emotional life. Both Elinor and Marianne regulate feeling, although to wholly different ends. Both assign feeling to the realm of value, judgment and sense. 'Sense' must be seen, then, as the more inclusive term, neither opposed to nor incompatible with feeling *or* sensibility but containing them, even if uneasily. The central conflict in the novel does not lie between sense and sensibility but between the sensitive and insensitive behaviour that essentially good, sensible people are capable of.

The next three chapters elaborate upon the distinctions drawn in the first by presenting dialogues which illustrate perfectly the speakers' chief concerns. In Chapter II, Mr and Mrs John Dashwood reconsider what assistance to his sisters will fulfil his promise to his father. Increasingly selfish and ill-natured arguments are brought forward against any disbursement, and against the promise itself, until the obligation is all but eradicated. Austen accomplishes the whole with notable speed and dexterity, and the passage has been much admired. In the following chapters, Mrs Dashwood, Marianne and Elinor discuss Edward Ferrars' character, a subject as important to them all as money is to their nearest relatives. Juxtaposing these dialogues suggests that any faults Marianne and Mrs Dashwood may subsequently exhibit are to be measured against the monumental selfishness of the John Dashwoods. These chapters also establish that the novel's characteristic medium will be a reflective prose dedicated to making careful distinctions. Normally, even dialogue serves this end: Elinor frequently tries to qualify with her speeches the comprehensive and often undiscriminating judgment typical of Marianne's conversation. Chapter IV opens with Marianne's 'What a pity it is . . . that Edward should have no taste for drawing,' and Elinor's careful reply:

> why should you think so? He does not draw himself, indeed, but he has great pleasure in seeing the performances of other people, and I assure you he is by no means deficient in natural taste, though he has not had opportunities of improving it. Had he ever been in the way of learning, I think he would have drawn very well. He distrusts his own judgment in such matters so much, that he is always unwilling to give his opinion on any picture; but he has an innate propriety and simplicity of taste, which in general direct him perfectly right (19).

Such speeches give Elinor a reputation for sententiousness which Marianne deserves at least as much, although this is seldom acknowledged; the phrase, 'that natural taste for your favourite pursuit which must be so indispensably necessary to your future felicity' (22) is, after all, Marianne's.

The most important function of the conversations in Chapters III and IV is, however, to introduce some themes central to the development. Among them is the influence of charm and physical attractiveness upon judgment. Marianne points to this motif when she concludes her amusing list of her requirements for a husband with, 'He must have all Edward's virtues, and his person and manners must ornament his goodness with every possible charm' (18). A character like Edward Ferrars, who lacks 'graces of person or address' (15), is particularly liable to disparagement unless some other charm operates; Mrs Dashwood's appreciation of his merits is 'perhaps assisted' by her 'persuasion of his regard for Elinor' (16). Marianne's judgment is less pliant: she loves Edward, but

> there is a something wanting – his figure is not striking; it has none of that grace which I should expect in the man who could seriously attach my sister. His eyes want all that spirit, that fire, which at once announce virtue and intelligence. And besides all this, I am afraid, mama, he has no real taste. Music seems scarcely to attract him, and though he admires Elinor's drawings very much, it is not the admiration of a person who can understand their worth. It is evident, in spite of his frequent attention to her while she draws, that in fact he knows nothing of the matter (17).

Marianne's denial of Edward's taste is reiterated and further explained in the next chapter: Edward's 'approbation' of drawing 'was very far from that rapturous delight, which, in her opinion, could alone be called taste' (19). This equation of 'rapturous delight' with taste derives from literary convention, and many of Marianne's other ideas about people, emotions and conduct spring from this same source, notably her opinion that second attachments are 'impossible' (56).

These ideas sometimes have an innocuous or merely amusing effect on Marianne's perceptions and conduct, but the consequences become more serious as the plot develops. The structure of the entire novel is based as much upon contrast and juxtaposition as are its opening chapters, for *Sense and Sensibility* depends upon a careful comparison of Elinor's and Marianne's conduct. The plot seems designed to observe even volume divisions in working out this comparison. Volume I establishes an elaborate parallel between Willoughby's and Edward's situations, underscoring the contrast between Elinor's and Marianne's conduct.

Both Willoughby and Edward are known to be dependent for sufficient income on the favour of an older female relative, and neither is justified in paying attentions to the Miss Dashwoods, Willoughby because he is 'trying to engage [Marianne's] regard, without a thought of returning it' (320), and Edward because he is engaged to another woman. More significant, however, is the manner in which the second volume (placed between the revelation to Elinor of Lucy's engagement and its revelation to the world at large) plays off Elinor's relations with Lucy against her relations with Marianne. Lucy's malice causes Elinor less acute suffering than does Marianne's blind, obtrusive misery.

Marianne's misery is obtrusive because her ideas about feeling, rooted in literary convention, encourage a self-indulgent display of her grief which constitutes an imposition on others. These ideas also generate a self-absorption which renders her imperceptive, insensitive and in the end unjust. The conversations on Edward's taste in Chapters III and IV offer the first hint that Marianne can perceive or attribute feeling only where it is expressed in her terms and according to her conventions. This quality is merely amusing when it makes her oblivious to Edward's taste for drawing or Colonel Brandon's for music: 'His pleasure in music, though it amounted not to that extatic delight which alone could sympathize with her own, was estimable when contrasted against the horrible insensibility of the others; and she was reasonable enough to allow that a man of five and thirty might well have outlived all acuteness of feeling and every exquisite power of enjoyment. She was perfectly disposed to make every allowance for the colonel's advanced state of life which humanity required' (35). More seriously, Marianne's blindness to others' feelings makes her misjudge Mrs Jennings, Colonel Brandon and, above all, Elinor.

Elinor's feelings and opinions are as strong as Marianne's, but she tries to allow for differences between her opinions and conduct and other people's, an allowance Marianne will not make. Discussing Willoughby's abrupt departure, Elinor remarks, 'In such a case, a plain and open avowal of his difficulties would have been more to his honour I think, as well as more consistent with his general character; – but I will not raise objections against any one's conduct on so illiberal a foundation, as a difference in judgement from myself, or a deviation from what I may think right and consistent' (81). Elinor is reluctant to judge others' conduct by her own standards exclusively; Marianne is unable to do otherwise. 'She expected from other people the same opinions and feelings as her own, and she judged of their motives by the immediate effect of their actions on herself' (202). Elinor would be made only more unhappy by the grief her mother and sisters would feel if they knew of Edward's engagement to Lucy: 'their tenderness and sorrow must add to her distress' (141). On the other hand, when Willoughby leaves Allenham, Marianne is shown 'indulging' her feelings and 'giving pain every moment to her mother and sisters, and forbidding all attempt at consolation from either. Her sensibility was potent enough!' (83).

Least excusable in Marianne's behaviour, however, is her injustice to Elinor, her propensity to underestimate and denigrate Elinor's feelings because they are not expressed as her own would be. Many instances can be adduced, but one long passage in particular makes perfectly explicit Elinor's feelings upon Edward's departure from Barton and Marianne's insensitivity to them:

> [Elinor] did not adopt the method so judiciously employed by Marianne, on a similar occasion, to augment and fix her sorrow, by seeking silence, solitude, and idleness. Their means were as different as their objects, and equally suited to the advancement of each.
>
> Elinor sat down to her drawing-table as soon as he was out of the house, busily employed herself the whole day, neither sought nor avoided the mention of his name, appeared to interest herself almost as much as ever in the general concerns of the family, and if, by this conduct, she did not lessen her own grief, it was at least prevented from unnecessary increase, and her mother and sisters were spared much solicitude on her account.
>
> Such behaviour as this, so exactly the reverse of her own, appeared no more meritorious to Marianne, than her own had seemed faulty to her. The business of self-command she settled very easily; – with strong affections it was impossible, with calm ones it could have no merit. That her sister's affections *were* calm, she dared not deny, though she blushed to acknowledge it; and of the strength of her own, she gave a very striking proof, by still loving and respecting that sister, in spite of this mortifying conviction.
>
> Without shutting herself up from her family, or leaving the house in determined solitude to avoid them, or lying awake the whole night to indulge meditation, Elinor found every day afforded her leisure enough to think of Edward, and of Edward's behaviour, in every possible variety which the different state of her spirits at different times could produce; – with tenderness, pity, approbation, censure, and doubt (104–5).

That Marianne is so incapable of correctly perceiving and estimating

Elinor's feelings gives considerable poignancy to the novel. This poignancy becomes sharper as the strength and complexity of Elinor's feelings are increasingly insisted on and increasingly rendered, as in the last line of this passage. If anything more were needed to attest the depth of her feelings, Elinor is, after all, able to judge and forgive Edward and Marianne, to love them and feel for their sufferings (for Edward's misery over his engagement), even while their thoughtlessness is causing her severe pain.

Although at the end of *Sense and Sensibility* both Marianne and Mrs Dashwood recognize that they have been insensitive to Elinor and inconsiderate of her feelings, their acknowledgment does not affect the novel's central perception that obtrusive, self-indulgent feeling will receive more attention and sympathy than will its opposite. This observation on the nature of emotional life is central to *Sense and Sensibility*, but Austen takes care to make certain others. She is, first of all, impatient with the notion that undying, unalterable feeling is possible or admirable in life or in literature, a notion which gives rise to Marianne's doctrine of the impossibility of second attachments and to Elinor's explicit rebuttal of it: 'And after all, Marianne, after all that is bewitching in the idea of a single and constant attachment, and all that can be said of one's happiness depending entirely on any particular person, it is not meant – it is not fit – it is not possible that it should be so' (263). One of Austen's letters declares that 'it is no creed of mine . . . that such sort of Disappointments [in love] kill anybody' (*L*, p. 411). Furthermore, she is aware that people who are suffering are as useless and painful to themselves as to others, and she considers that exertion of strength to appear as if one is not suffering is not only possible but imperative: such exertion ensures that pain will be neither unnecessarily increased nor tainted by affectation.

To exert oneself in this manner is to conform to social convention, fulfilling the tacit obligation not to embarrass or distress others uselessly with one's own misery. Such exertion is neither hypocritical nor heartless, even by modern standards; in these circumstances, obligations to others do not conflict with obligations to oneself. Yet, other suppressions seem to be dictated by convention only, such as the suppression of good feeling. When Elinor wishes that Marianne's and Willoughby's attachment 'were less openly shewn; and once or twice did venture to suggest the propriety of some self-command to Marianne' (53), social forms may seem to be rigidly and repressively enforced. Marianne's reply is especially attractive by comparison; she 'abhorred all concealment where no real disgrace could attend unreserve; and to aim at the restraint of sentiments which were not in themselves illaudable, appeared to her not merely an unnecessary effort, but a disgraceful subjection of reason to common-place and mistaken notions' (53).

It is easy to be convinced by this apparent defence of openness and unreserve and to be repelled by Elinor's complaint that Marianne's 'systems have all the unfortunate tendency of setting propriety at nought' (56). To respond in this way is, however, to overlook Elinor's (and Austen's) real objection to Marianne's conduct: not that it is too 'open', but that it is too selfish. In displaying their affection for each other at the expense of 'general politeness' (49), Marianne and Willoughby rudely ignore the claims of others. When Sir John Middleton asks, 'Where is Marianne? Has she run away because we are come?' (105), Austen registers the unattractiveness of Marianne's habitual rudeness. The alternative modes of social behaviour at issue are not, after all, prudent, cautious reserve on the one hand and warm-hearted, spontaneous openness on the other. Reserve, deceit and even the worst kind of prudence lie behind Willoughby's apparently open affection for Marianne. He is first trifling with her happiness, and then with his own, as his final revelation to Elinor makes clear:

> Even *then*, however, when fully determined on paying my addresses to her, I allowed myself most improperly to put off, from day to day, the moment of doing it, from an unwillingness to enter into an engagement while my circumstances were so greatly embarrassed. I will not reason here – nor will I stop for *you* to expatiate on the absurdity . . . of scrupling to engage my faith where my honour was already bound. The event has proved, that I was a cunning fool, providing with great circumspection for a possible opportunity of making myself contemptible and wretched for ever (321).

Furthermore, Marianne's and Willoughby's display of feeling is not really spontaneous at all: they are open on principle; their behaviour is self-conscious, governed by their own rules or conventions: 'their behaviour, at all times, was an illustration of their opinions' (53). Spontaneity, however, is unwilled; and Marianne can voluntarily check 'the spontaneous overflow of powerful feelings' when she chooses, that is, when her principles or standards are threatened. She deplores jargon, so she sometimes keeps to herself her feelings about a picturesque scene 'because I could find no language to describe them in but what was worn and hackneyed out of all sense and meaning' (97). When she yields to her grief at leaving Norland or at Willoughby's leaving Allenham, she is guilty of some affectation in working up her feelings. That her displays of feeling are completely self-conscious and even regulated becomes clear when she is compared to a character like Catherine Morland, who *is* perfectly naïve and spontaneous. She does reveal her affection for Henry Tilney openly and unconsciously, and is certainly not censured for it.

In *Sense and Sensibility*, the reader is presented with two modes of regulating feeling. Elinor governs the expression of her feelings according to social conventions, Marianne according to literary conventions. Austen dramatizes throughout the novel the consequences in conduct and feeling of each mode. She shows that conventional, polite behaviour which dictates the control of feeling is based on a truer perception of the nature of emotions than are the conventions of sensibility: social conventions permit and assist emotions like grief to become attenuated by natural processes, while the doctrines of sensibility undermine or falsify real feeling by seeking to perpetuate or increase it. In *Sense and Sensibility*, social conventions are an advantage to the self, assisting and supporting the fulfilment of personality, because at their best they codify careful, responsive and responsible consideration for the feelings of other people. They do not constitute ends in themselves but rather the readiest and most reliable means to construct those habits of consideration which Austen most values and trusts. She is convinced that habits of feeling, of response and of conduct are more desirable and more solid than impulses, and that they therefore deserve attention whether character is to be formed or judged. These views of social convention and emotional life, however commonplace they may have been to Austen's contemporaries, are less usual now; and certainly their singularity helps to account for the generally unfavourable reception accorded *Sense and Sensibility*. But Austen's views are not necessarily alienating or wholly foreign. Real feeling, she declares, brings together private and public experience, or one's relations with oneself and with others. Real feeling goes deeper than manners and morals and conduct; it supplies the foundation upon which they should be constructed. Real feeling defines and fulfils personality; without it, the self is deformed and deadened.

These perceptions, like the others, are embodied in *Sense and Sensibility* through contrasts among the characters, and lend themselves to this technique quite neatly, indeed, somewhat schematically. To examine social convention in relation to feeling is to examine degrees of good breeding (manners or propriety) in relation to degrees of good nature; and various degrees of sense can be used to complicate the scheme. The single chapter (i, vii) which introduces Sir John and Lady Middleton, Mrs Jennings and Colonel Brandon, and those subsequent chapters which make known the Palmers and describe the responses of all these characters to Marianne's suffering, show the qualities of sense and silliness, good and ill nature, and good and ill breeding, in several combinations. Good breeding is consistent with coldness and ill nature in Lady Middleton. Ill breeding is, in Sir John and Mrs Palmer, consistent with good nature and with varying degrees of silliness; and it is coupled in Mrs Jennings with good nature and a certain shrewdness. Ill-bred behaviour finally shows itself to be compatible with the ill nature and the sense of Mr Palmer. Only Colonel Brandon is sensible, good-natured and well-bred. These contrasts suggest that good feelings, such as those of Mrs Jennings, Sir John and Charlotte Palmer, do not necessarily result in truly 'feeling' behaviour, and that the insensitivity and indifference of a Lady Middleton may more closely approximate 'feeling' behaviour simply because it is well-bred behaviour: 'The calm and polite unconcern of Lady Middleton on the occasion was an happy relief to Elinor's spirits, oppressed as they often were by the clamorous kindness of the others.... Every qualification is raised at times, by the circumstances of the moment, to more than its real value; and she was sometimes worried down by officious condolence to rate good-breeding as more indispensable to comfort than good-nature' (215).

Considerate behaviour does not necessarily follow from the wish to be considerate. An ability to determine what will be most acceptable and most helpful to others' feelings is required. This determination is never easy. It challenges even those who are 'feeling', sensible and good-natured, like Colonel Brandon. In undertaking to expose Willoughby to Marianne, Colonel Brandon questions his motives, uncertain whether he is concerned principally to assist Marianne or to forward his own suit by undermining Marianne's esteem for Willoughby. The difficulties and anxieties which inevitably accompany sensitivity to others' feelings and consciousness of one's own are reflected even in the syntax of his speech to Elinor: ' "My regard for her, for yourself, for your mother – will you allow me to prove it, by relating some circumstances, which nothing but a *very* sincere regard – nothing but an earnest desire of being useful – I think I am justified – though where so many hours have been spent in convincing myself that I am right, is there not some reason to fear I may be wrong?'' He stopped' (204).

Colonel Brandon's narrative contains all the stock elements of interpolated histories like that of Caroline Evelyn in Fanny Burney's *Evelina*. Colonel Brandon recounts his love for his cousin, her forced marriage to his brother, her subsequent seduction and desertion, the birth of her illegitimate child, her squalid and penitent deathbed on which she confides her child Eliza to his care, and finally, Eliza's parallel fate: she has been seduced and deserted by Willoughby. This history is usually dismissed as dull and hackneyed, but it has a significant place in Austen's system of contrasts, and functions adequately there. The narrative resolves the contrasts between him and Willoughby which are initiated by one of the most obviously symmetrical of the chapters. In it, Elinor's, Marianne's and Mrs Dashwood's estimations of Willoughby are compared with each other and then juxtaposed with an argument between Elinor, Marianne and Willoughby on Colonel Brandon's character. Implicit in the chapter is the contrast between Colonel Brandon's age, gravity and reserve, and Willoughby's youth, liveliness and 'ardour of mind' (48). Colonel Brandon's history indicates, however, that he has been a victim of a first attachment. In this and in the mysterious melancholy he exhibits until his revelation, Colonel Brandon and not Willoughby is the conventional romantic hero; Willoughby is simply, sordidly (and conventionally too), a libertine. Austen amuses herself with this ironic contrast and with a fairly simple ironic consequence: Colonel Brandon's romantic qualities are wholly unattractive to Marianne, even though, as Elinor says, 'her opinions are all romantic'(56).

At certain points in her narrative, Austen moves beyond her technique of contrast and her visible and consistent patterning of events, in order to assemble characters and to produce scenes and confrontations which prefigure the confrontations found in the later novels and there so justly admired. She does not in *Sense and Sensibility* completely control or exploit the device, as the dinner at Mrs John Dashwood's London residence amply illustrates. It does not bear comparison with those scenes at Box Hill, Sotherton or the White Hart, which convey below the surface of polite or idle talk the cross-currents of passion, misapprehension, vanity, awareness or ugliness (sometimes approaching evil) which make up emotional life. Although the feelings and designs of the dinner guests are sufficiently at odds with each other to produce considerable pain among them – and in fact some pain is registered – a comic tone is sustained. Little sense of the strain of conflicting emotions is communicated.

Something of ugliness does appear in the more moving, more successful confrontation managed between Elinor and Lucy Steele, which occurs after Lucy has forced upon Elinor a knowledge of her engagement to Edward. Elinor wishes to 'pump' Lucy, to draw her out and to probe her feelings for Edward; accordingly, Lucy exposes herself completely. Lucy hopes to torment Elinor with an account of Edward's love, and to tempt her into the false position of advising her, Lucy, to give up Edward. Consequently, Lucy's remarks become increasingly unpleasant and pointed; and Elinor responds with a phrase – 'two people so tenderly attached' (150) – that constitutes, in context, a sharp dig at Lucy. Elinor's real feelings come out. Emotion cannot always be suppressed even though habit, interest (one's own advantage, in this case the satisfaction of not letting Lucy know her power to hurt) and politeness all dictate it. Austen does not deny to emotion a life of its own: she acknowledges its power and its assertion of independence at the same time that she indicates that human, civilized behaviour depends upon checking, guiding and harnessing it. The tension between these imperatives animates the most important scenes in her novels, and gives strength to her themes and vitality to her plots. That a narrow and mean consciousness like Lady Middleton's can to some extent produce the civilized and feeling behaviour Austen tries to describe is noted with honesty and with amusement, but her conviction of the value of that behaviour remains unshaken.

Observations of this kind are necessary if *Sense and Sensibility* is to be fairly and accurately evaluated, and if the common charges that it is inflexible and 'rigid' are to be met. These charges, which condemn the novel to narrowness and over-simplicity, proceed from a judgment that its terms are too strictly defined and too consistently adhered to. The novel is thus considered not only flatly mechanical, but sterile and unmoving. Both these accusations are false to one's sense of the novel's vitality, its power to portray and to engage human feeling.

The charge of static, mechanical movement in the action is the more formidable because it is closer to the truth. Austen *does* adhere to the patterns of contrast she sets up, and the patterns are remarkably visible. But if the argument is accepted that her subject is not 'sense' versus 'sensibility' or 'sense' reconciling itself with 'sensibility', but rather a study of sensitive behaviour – what assists or militates against it and what it costs – then it is clear that her 'tags' do not indicate or limit the meaning of the novel. In this light, the contrasts and heavy patterning seem to be Austen's delight rather than her burden: she is exploring and enjoying the possibilities of formal symmetry. Her parallels and contrasts have an exuberant quality in their proclaimed and assertive character. She calls attention, here as in *Northanger Abbey* and *Pride and Prejudice*, to her own technical virtuosity, her own mastery of the principles of structure. Her later novels are more subtly organized. Technique is so mastered that the difficulty those novels present lies precisely in isolating technique and detaching it from its material. There, technique approaches invisibility – a condition appropriate enough to the more complex, more delicate and more penetrating perceptions of those novels. The brilliance and clarity of the early novels, their greater openness and accessibility, derive largely from the exuberance and obtrusiveness of their techniques.

If Austen's technique is acquitted of sterility, it does not necessarily follow that her subject matter deserves similar acquittal: it may be lifeless, even though the devices which shape it are not used lifelessly. Does the creation of Elinor, a character who does not need to correct herself, deprive *Sense and Sensibility* of all tension, all development or, more to the point, of all possibility of evoking emotional response? It is true that Elinor's relation to herself is essentially static; but in her relations to other people she is embattled and tested. A central source of tension in the novel is that Elinor must cope with the rudeness and insensitivity of her associates – not only of Lucy (which is minimally disrupting) but of those she loves best, her mother and Marianne – without succumbing to self-pity or self-righteousness, and without ceasing to be, herself, sensitive to and considerate of them. She does complain, but seldom and quietly. As a result, when Marianne's recovery from illness is assured, 'the brilliant cheerfulness of Mrs Dashwood's looks and spirits proved her to be, as she repeatedly declared herself, one of the happiest women in the world. Elinor could not hear the declaration, nor witness its proofs without sometimes wondering whether her mother ever recollected Edward' (335). The long speech in which Elinor describes what her feelings have been in response to Edward's engagement, to the malice of Lucy, Mrs Ferrars and Mrs John Dashwood, and to Marianne's unhappiness, in order to correct Marianne's supposition that she has never 'felt much', is her most explicit complaint, and is certainly called for by Marianne's injustice, yet it avoids bitterness and blame; its tone is poignant.

For four months, Marianne, I have had all this hanging on my mind, without being at liberty to speak of it to a single creature; knowing that it would make you and my mother most unhappy whenever it were explained to you, yet unable to prepare you for it in the least. – It was told me, – it was in a manner forced on me by the very person herself, whose prior engagement ruined all my prospects; and told me, as I thought, with triumph. – This person's suspicions, therefore, I have had to oppose, by endeavouring to appear indifferent where I have been most deeply interested; – and it has not been only once; – I have had her hopes and exultation to listen to again and again. – I have known myself to be divided from Edward for ever, without hearing one circumstance that could make me less desire the connection. – Nothing has proved him unworthy; nor has any thing declared him indifferent to me. – I have had to contend against the unkindness of his sister, and the insolence of his mother; and have suffered the punishment of an attachment, without enjoying its advantages. – And all this has been going on at a time, when, as you too well know, it has not been my only unhappiness. – If you can think me capable of ever feeling – surely you may suppose that I have suffered *now*. The composure of mind with which I have brought myself at present to consider the matter, the consolation that I have been willing to admit, have been the effect of constant and painful exertion; – they did not spring up of themselves; – they did not occur to relieve my spirits at first – No, Marianne. – *Then*, if I had not been bound to silence, perhaps nothing could have kept me entirely – not even what I owed to my dearest friends – from openly shewing that I was *very* unhappy (263–4).

That Elinor has to say such things is painful enough, but worse, she speaks in vain. Marianne does not become less insensitive to her as a result of this speech, and the same must be said of some of the novel's readers. Perhaps Elinor simply does not complain enough. But Austen does in the end sufficiently render the poignancy of Elinor's situations – with Edward and Lucy, and with Marianne and her mother. That poignancy is the characteristic note of the novel, and, rendered quietly and carefully, it is prevented both in Elinor herself and in the novel as a whole from being sentimentalized into self-indulgence or moralized into self-righteousness.

3. CONTROL OF JUDGMENT AND SYMPATHY

In depth of emotional content and in complexity of themes and design, *Sense and Sensibility* clearly represents a considerable advance on *Northanger Abbey*. Its most significant contribution to the development of Austen's art, however, lies in its treatment of the responses of judgment and sympathy. Austen attempts in *Sense and Sensibility* to manipulate and finally to educate these responses in her readers. Her interest is, as might be expected, principally engaged by sympathy, and central to her view of it as an emotional response is its refractoriness. Sympathy is either too ready to hand in particular cases, or in others too inert. She intends in her novels to work against this refractoriness and correct it somewhat. She entertains no great opinion of its corrigibility, having so keen an awareness of the limitations of human emotional responsiveness, but she does consider that the response of sympathy can, at least, profit by becoming aware of itself, by perceiving its own problematic nature.

In *Sense and Sensibility*, sympathetic responses are both described in the novel's action and elicited and exercised by it. Elinor's and Marianne's responsiveness to each other and to other characters in the novel is presented, and in turn the reader's responses to them are engaged. Responsiveness to other characters in an Austen novel is expected to issue in, or at least to include, some judgment of them, both by the characters themselves and by the reader. Although Austen never suspends the activity of judgment, she concerns herself with portraying its complicated, inextricable linkage with feeling, particularly with sympathy. 'Pure' judgment does not exist. Sympathies and biases always and inevitably qualify it, and for this reason the educating, the directing and the enriching of sympathy become all the more important. Thus Elinor's judgment of Edward's behaviour is, quite explicitly, more liberal than her judgment of Willoughby's. Her love for Edward engages her sympathy and thereby her favourable judgment: 'Disappointed, however, and vexed as she was, and sometimes displeased with his uncertain behaviour to herself, she was very well disposed on the whole to regard his actions with all the candid allowances and generous qualifications, which had been rather more painfully extorted from her, for Willoughby's service, by her mother' (101). When she does feel sympathy for Willoughby after his confession, her response is largely created by qualities which appeal to feelings rather than to judgment: 'She felt that his influence over her mind was heightened by circumstances which ought not in reason to have weight; by that person of uncommon attraction, that open, affectionate, and lively manner which it was no merit to possess; and by that still ardent love for Marianne, which it was not even innocent to indulge. But she felt that it was so, long, long before she could feel his influence less' (333).

Attractiveness, energy and charm inevitably influence judgment by affecting feeling. Austen's very keen awareness of these facts may not be unique, but without it she certainly would not be a novelist, nor be qualified to explore emotional and moral life. Her perception of the frequent irrationality, even injustice, of sympathy, and of its occasionally gratuitous nature, balances a perception of its equally unreasonable and unjust inactivity in good, well-disposed people, exemplified in the lack of sympathy accorded Elinor by her mother and Marianne. That Austen's perceptions are perfectly accurate and perfectly descriptive of the tendencies of emotional responsiveness in general has been amply attested by some of her critics: they are charmed by Marianne and Willoughby; they are alienated by Elinor. But these tendencies in readers are meant to be, and ought to be, redirected by the text. The reader should become conscious first, that enthusiasm and sympathy for sheer charm and liveliness often induce blindness to what lies beneath the charm, and second, that the absence of brilliance or flamboyance – in, for instance, Elinor – will often immobilize, or at least discourage, the flow of sympathy. *Mansfield Park*, which shares some of the themes and concerns of *Sense and Sensibility*, demands an almost identical consciousness from its readers in relation to Fanny Price and the Crawfords.

In *Sense and Sensibility*, Austen leaves charm to take care of itself: she is aware that it has the least to fear from injustice and from lack of response. Her method with Elinor is different – and remarkable, considering that her own sympathies are most strongly engaged by her. She refuses to elicit for Elinor any sympathy independent of a cool, clear perception – a judgment – of her role in the action. In what she requires of herself as a novelist in this her first conceived and published novel, Austen exhibits a stern control perfectly in accord with the stringent vision she unfolds. The injustice which Elinor encounters is presented calmly and unportentously. It excites no bitterness or indignation, either in Elinor herself or in the narrator. Generated instead is a sharp, clear, harsh but also rather amused, awareness that unobtrusive suffering will be met with unjust, unfeeling behaviour. Sympathy for Elinor depends upon and derives from this rational apprehension of her position. Austen intends to create, and does create in the reader's response to Elinor, an interdependence between sympathy and judgment. These are made, of necessity, to work together. One gives rise to the other, in precisely the way that they operate in Elinor's own consciousness.

In *Sense and Sensibility*, Austen first gives form to her most characteristic theme, the educating of the judgment and sympathy. The novel lacks, however, many of the techniques later developed to engage and control these responses. It is not as highly structured as *Pride and Prejudice*. Austen has not yet fully developed the technique of linear irony, which she perfects in *Pride and Prejudice*. This technique complicates all the novels after *Sense and Sensibility* and contributes largely to their density and power. In *Pride and Prejudice*, most of the incidents and dialogue, and all of the wit, are governed by linear irony; this cannot be said of the earlier novel. When incidents involving misjudgments or misapprehensions occur in *Sense and Sensibility*, the mistakes are in general quickly recognized and registered; or if not, their effect on the action is minimal. Comedy or poignancy is the usual result of these misapprehensions. Their effects are immediate rather than cumulative. Elinor's mistaken conviction that Edward's ring contains a lock of her hair is soon enough followed by her discovery that Edward is engaged and the hair is Lucy's. Her mistake is not significant to the scheme: no real consequences follow. In the same way, when Lucy begins to reveal her engagement, Elinor first supposes that Edward's brother Robert must be meant, and her lack of delight 'with the idea of such a sister-in-law' (129) is immediately dispelled by Lucy's announcement that she is betrothed to Edward. This incident is neither recalled nor felt at the end when Lucy has married Robert Ferrars and Elinor has married Edward. In *Pride and Prejudice*, however, every incident involving judgment is cumulative. Austen learns to extract more from her material than she can in *Sense and Sensibility*, where only the treatment of Elinor and Marianne creates a cumulative effect and where many incidents contribute nothing to the rendering of their characters. For instance, no adverse or ironic comment on the characters' failure to detect Willoughby's shallowness, mercenariness and libertinism is implied at any point, however the failure is regretted; Austen's treatment of Elizabeth Bennet's misjudgments of Wickham and Darcy is altogether different. The reader of *Sense and Sensibility* is given no opportunity to dissociate himself from Elinor's, Marianne's and Mrs Dashwood's favourable judgments of Willoughby, whereas *Pride and Prejudice* presents a reader with sufficient hints that he ought to judge differently from Elizabeth at certain points, even as Austen contrives to make it unlikely that he will do so.

Sense and Sensibility addresses itself to the unruliness of sympathy rather than judgment, as in *Pride and Prejudice*, or rather than of both, as in *Mansfield Park*. This claim depends on recognizing delicate shades of emphasis, for Austen's constant theme is that the operations of the two responses are inextricable, however ludicrous or inappropriate the result. In *Sense and Sensibility*, however, she interests herself in exploring feeling or sympathy in relation to conduct rather than to judgment. She wishes to define genuinely feeling behaviour or conduct and to promote genuine responsiveness, not just to literature but to other people as well. The relations of judgment and sympathy explored in the later novels are, however, by nature far more problematic as well as more profound than the relations between feeling and conduct – although perhaps hardly more important. The 'sympathy' those novels describe and elicit becomes a more judicious, more complex and consequently, more intimate response, quite different from either the enthusiasm generated by Marianne or the calm, rueful poignancy evoked by Elinor. Finally, the two responses of judgment and sympathy are presented in simple interaction (in the reader's, and at last in Marianne's, response to Elinor's predicament) or in simple opposition (in the reader's and Elinor's response to Marianne, who elicits affection and adverse judgment simultaneously). The reader, experiencing responses thus combined and complicated, enriches his emotional and moral consciousness.

3 *Pride and Prejudice* and its Predecessors

Pride and Prejudice occupies a central position among Austen's works. It is the last and most complex of the early novels. It was considerably revised just prior to, or possibly even during, the composition of *Mansfield Park* (which represents a remarkable advance), yet it incorporates some of her earliest concerns, themes and techniques. A preliminary approach to these themes and techniques must be made through the fiction of Austen's predecessors, for of all her novels, *Pride and Prejudice* includes the most embedded, insistent and interesting links to earlier fiction. Too often discussions of the relations to forerunners merely cite the numerous parallel incidents or plots. Lascelles has once and for all defined the uselessness of such efforts: 'to find an episode or turn of plot in one of Jane Austen's novels which resembles one in some earlier novel–even though that precursor should be one of her favourites, and prompting be as likely an explanation as coincidence–*this* tells us very little of what the work of that earlier novelist meant to Jane Austen; for, so long as she remained content to build her plots of these major incidents, she could not but build them of material that had been used already'.[1] The difficulty, then, lies in locating parallels which *can* be explained by 'prompting', not 'coincidence', parallels which have intention behind them and which, therefore, point to interesting and illuminating relationships between the methods and intentions of Austen's fiction and that of her predecessors. She is known to have liked best among them Maria Edgeworth, Fanny Burney and above all, the Samuel Richardson of *Sir Charles Grandison* (a rather surprising selection to modern taste). Although all these writers are less successful in the attempt than she, all can be observed trying, like her, to deal with the problem of the reader's response to fiction, trying to find literary means to elicit and control this response for didactic purposes. The important question is how and why these generally unrealized attempts and purposes of earlier authors become moving and compelling in Austen's works. An answer can be approached by studying the two novels which have a special relation to *Pride and Prejudice* and which anticipate and to some extent share its purposes: *Cecilia, or Memoirs of an*

Heiress (1782), in which Burney abandons the epistolary form adopted for *Evelina*; and *Sir Charles Grandison* (1753–4), a novel-in-letters.

1. *CECILIA*

That Burney's intentions or achievements share anything with Austen's has usually been denied, although the relation between them is frequently discussed. Austen's interest in *Cecilia* and her esteem for it are demonstrated in a well-known passage from *Northanger Abbey*: ' "It is only Cecilia, or Camilla, or Belinda;" or, in short, only some work in which the greatest powers of the mind are displayed, in which the most thorough knowledge of human nature, the happiest delineation of its varieties, the liveliest effusions of wit and humour are conveyed to the world in the best chosen language' (38). Although no contemporary critic can fully accept this assessment, the important question is, are there elements in *Cecilia* which would justify Austen's praise and which might have inspired her, other than fairly superficial and unhelpful ones like the phrase 'pride and prejudice'? The phrase should not be dismissed altogether; close examination of Burney's treatment of 'pride' yields surprising results. The relation between the two novels has been explored by several critics, largely because what is usually taken as the moral of Cecilia may have supplied the title, *Pride and Prejudice*. Although other possible sources for the title exist ('the phrase must be regarded as a commonplace'[2]) various resemblances (either parallel or contrasting) to the incidents and characters of *Cecilia* suggest that some relation is present and meant to be noted.

At first glance, the plot of *Cecilia* suggests only differences from *Pride and Prejudice*. Cecilia Beverley, beautiful, intelligent and prudent, has inherited £3000 a year from her uncle, but she will lose this fortune unless the man she marries takes her name. Her uncle's death has left her in the care of three guardians: the profligate and spendthrift Harrel, the miser Briggs and the proud and prejudiced elder Mr Delvile. At the start of the novel, Cecilia moves to London to reside with Mr Harrel and his wife, a weak, silly former schoolmate. During her residence there, which occupies the first half of the novel, she is introduced to society. Her financial generosity is tested by worthy and unworthy suppliants and the unworthy among them partially overcome her prudence. She meets her third guardian's wife and son, Mrs Delvile and Mortimer Delvile, and she falls in love with Mortimer. Both Mrs Delvile and her son think Cecilia engaged to someone else and consequently think themselves safe, since both reject the idea of Delvile's giving up his name. All three are seen estimating, and misinterpreting, each other.

The second half of the novel begins, symmetrically enough, with Cecilia's taking up residence for a time at Delvile Castle, because her former guardian, Harrel, having wasted his own and a portion of Cecilia's fortune, has committed suicide. In this half of the novel, Cecilia's emotional generosity and honour are tried; from here on, pride and prejudice are shown to conflict with the love Mrs Delvile, Delvile and Cecilia feel for each other. Delvile at last reveals his love to Cecilia by various means and Cecilia reveals hers subsequently, and fortuitously, to him. A clandestine marriage is attempted and (in a typically Burneyan combination) thwarted by coincidence, by the plots of Mr Monckton, who wants to marry Cecilia, and by Cecilia's own misgivings and guilt and pride. At last the climactic scene occurs: Mrs Delvile, a character in whom Fanny Burney intended to blend 'noble and rare qualities with striking and incurable defects',[3] tries to prevent the marriage (which outrages her family pride) by working on the pride of both Cecilia and her son. She succeeds, but is brought some months later to sanction a private marriage between them, as a result of the willingness of all three to renounce Cecilia's fortune in order to preserve the Delvile name. The marriage takes place secretly and is followed by an immediate separation, for Mortimer Delvile and Mrs Delvile go to the Continent. This separation leaves Cecilia prey to the distresses experienced by every eighteenth-century heroine after Clarissa, and she suffers in rapid succession the loss of her home, her money, her health and her reason, all as a result of her false position: her clandestine and unacknowledged marriage. At last, a final reunion with Delvile takes place, and health and reason and even fortune are restored. Although Cecilia's original fortune is irrevocably lost, Burney cannot resist bequeathing her, almost immediately, another fortune in her own right from Mrs Delvile's sister.

Perhaps because of the considerable surface differences, most critics have restricted themselves to finding rather narrow resemblances or obvious contrasts. For example, Mrs Bennet's vulgarity, embarrassing to Elizabeth, is likened to Mrs Belfield's, embarrassing to her daughter and to Cecilia. Or the central scene in *Cecilia*, in which Mrs Delvile appeals to Cecilia to renounce Mortimer for the sake of his family pride, is often contrasted to the very different scene in *Pride and Prejudice* between Elizabeth and Lady Catherine de Bourgh. But noting such parallels and contrasts does not really account for or describe the connection most readers sense between the novels, and between the works of Austen and

Burney generally. That relation remains difficult to define, apart from the clear and universal judgment that Austen's novels are much better.

Q.D. Leavis is one of the few critics who has formulated a theory of the relationship: *Pride and Prejudice* began as an 'anti-*Cecilia*,' a *Cecilia* made realistic, and was later expanded to an examination of marriage, 'the marriage of love in the face of family disapprobation', and its 'obverse', 'the marriage of convenience that is approved by worldly wisdom'. She concludes that *Pride and Prejudice* 'is the central idea of *Cecilia* given an elaborate orchestration',[4] but her account is unsatisfactory. The two forms of marriage that Leavis mentions, though discussed in both novels, do not constitute the 'central idea' of either. Nor does the tag 'pride and prejudice' suggest the theme of either novel adequately. Although Burney does allow one character to speak of 'pride and prejudice' as the motive of the action, and although she does refer to prejudice at intervals in *Cecilia*, she uses the word in a very narrow sense, as an adjunct to pride: prejudice in favour of one's own name or class. Attempts to define what the two novels do share in theme must examine the terms 'pride and prejudice' more deeply, and finally go beyond them.

Prejudice in its wider sense, implying the problem of judgment, *is* present in *Cecilia* but not under that name. Burney is interested in misjudgment, and even in demonstrating its origins in pride, but she treats misjudgment as only one of the unfortunate effects of pride. Thus, the pride of the Delviles can offend Cecilia's own pride and cause her to react coldly and distantly, so that misunderstandings follow, and pride is involved in Cecilia's and Delvile's eagerness to misinterpret and think the worst of each other. These misjudgments, however, are less the result of pride than of the irritations and anxieties of love which is unacknowledged at first, even to themselves, and later thwarted. Burney makes no real attempt to connect the operations of judgment with the operations of pride. Pride is her central theme and she explores it in a fine eighteenth-century manner, combining it schematically with different qualities in her characters. Mr Belfield, for example, unites pride with imprudence and Mr Monckton, his opposite number, unites pride and the reverse, overcalculation. They are each, of course, brought to most exemplary ruin, although Belfield, the less guilty, is rescued at the end. In her diary, Burney summarizes her intentions: 'I merely meant to show how differently pride, like every other quality, operates upon different minds'.[5] Nevertheless, a more sophisticated and complex exploration of the workings of pride – its effects on other emotions and on judgment – can be found in *Cecilia* than the crudity of Burney's summary or the novel's style would lead the reader to expect. Austen does echo this schematic exploration of pride in parts of *Pride and Prejudice*, but the echo only emphasizes its subordinate position there.

Some interesting structural parallels do exist between the novels – which, however, serve finally to point up differences in technique. Most obviously, Cecilia's visit to Delvile Castle early in Book VI, the novel's midpoint, parallels Elizabeth's visit to Pemberley at the start of Volume III. Burney takes the usual opportunity to characterize an owner by his property, and the elder Mr Delvile's limitations are underscored by the castle's 'evident struggle to support some appearance of its ancient dignity, [which] made the dwelling and all in it's [sic] vicinity wear an aspect of constraint and austerity'.[6] Darcy's virtues are likewise suggested by the 'natural beauty . . . so little counteracted by an awkward taste' (245) and the 'real elegance' (246) of Pemberley. More important, both sets of lovers are brought together by these visits, and in the encounters which follow, the characters experience difficulty in determining one another's feelings, though each becomes gradually more sure of his own. The feelings of Elizabeth and Darcy are more complex than those of Cecilia and Delvile, yet similarities exist in the delineation of emotional tension and in the choice of a character's 'home grounds' to bring it out. Austen uses Darcy's inarticulateness and then his civility to show his feeling for Elizabeth; Burney has to invent crises (like a thunderstorm) so that Delvile's tenderness can show itself in anxiety. Austen's parallel crisis – Lydia's elopement – shows her skill: the ambiguity of Darcy's response is only cleared up later, and the incident permits the fullest possible test of Darcy's generosity and feeling by allowing him to effect Lydia's marriage and then become the 'Brother-in-law of Wickham'! Elizabeth herself reflects, 'Every kind of pride must revolt from the connection' (326). Typically, Darcy's response upon hearing of the elopement, 'walking up and down the room in earnest meditation; his brow contracted, his air gloomy' (278), is far less melodramatic and contrived than Delvile's response to Cecilia's supposed danger from the storm: ' "[Your life] is more precious," cried he with vehemence, "than the air I breathe!" and seizing her hand, he drew it under his arm, and, without waiting her consent, almost forced her away with him' (VI, v; III, 268). Both responses are stilted and conventional by comparison with the gestures Austen later uses to convey feeling, such as Captain Wentworth's silently removing her nephew from Anne Elliot's neck in *Persuasion* (80) or Mr Knightley's flush accompanying his answer, made while 'hard at work' buttoning his shoes, to Emma's hint that he loves Jane Fairfax (287).

A significant parallelism in structure is provided by the author's common interest in contriving linear irony, by systematically organizing the action to undercut the characters' and the readers' expectations. Thus, the overall ironic structure of Cecilia – in which the heiress becomes a penniless bride and demonstrates that fortune, beauty and intelligence united do not guarantee happiness – is intended to violate the contemporary reader's expectations. Similarly, Cecilia's own over-confidence in her ability to predict and control her feelings (such as falling in love) and her later smug certainty that Delvile's delay in proposing to her springs merely from his uncertainty of success, are very decidedly contradicted by the action. Although linear irony is a major structural element in *Pride and Prejudice*, Austen's different uses of the device are notable, particularly as epitomized by the distinction between the ironic rebuke arranged for Elizabeth's 'pride of judgment' (her judgments are shown to err again and again) and the irony of the rational Cecilia's temporarily losing her reason at the end. Burney's irony, however, is largely superficial or external; Austen's is motivated by character.

The difference is echoed in each author's use of the basic and familiar courtship pattern to structure her novel. The courtship novel depends on inventing obstacles to marriage, obstacles which are typically 'external' in the works of Burney and the early works of Austen. Already in *Sense and Sensibility*, however, the marriages prevented by outside influences are not those which resolve the plot, but rather those between Edward and Lucy Steele, and Willoughby and Marianne. A transition to emphasis on plausible or 'internal' rather than contrived obstacles is already evident: Edward's foolish engagement to Lucy delays his marriage to Elinor, and Willoughby's mercenariness together with his seduction of Miss Williams make a marriage to Marianne impossible. This transition to the use of internal obstacles is furthered by *Pride and Prejudice* (Lady Catherine is an ineffectual remnant of earlier external obstacles) and completed by the later novels, in which the central couples have been long acquainted, and which therefore tend to show love unaware of itself or unacknowledged love becoming aware.

Burney's artificial and contrived obstacles do cause internal conflicts, so they are not wholly lacking in thematic interest. She likes to arrange and show conflicts between love and other feelings (the conflict between love and 'pride and prejudice' is inescapable in eighteenth-century literature) and, even more conventionally, between love and duty or reason or principle – including the 'principle' that a lady must not love someone who does not love her. This rule, alluded to mockingly in *Northanger Abbey* (29–30) and notoriously formulated by Richardson in the *Rambler*, is not invariably adhered to even by *his* heroines: 'That a young lady should be in love, and the love of the young gentleman undeclared, is an heterodoxy which prudence, and even policy, must not allow.'[7] Austen's predecessors were interested in this problem. Burney's Cecilia and Edgeworth's Belinda, among others, experience conflict from the attempt to control their own feelings until they know those of their lovers. This is not utterly barren ground for a novelist. Some of Burney's best effects in *Cecilia* are rooted here, and Austen's treatment of Fanny Price and Anne Elliot shows how she can transform this stock material.

Clearly, the structural parallels between *Cecilia* and *Pride and Prejudice* underscore Austen's superior techniques. If these parallels accounted for every link between the novels, Austen's interest in *Cecilia* would remain inexplicable. But in Burney's attitude to her heroine Austen found much to interest her and to build on. First of all, Cecilia is not a faultless heroine; she has limits, and Burney treats them with irony. When Cecilia first discovers and admits that she loves Delvile, Burney is not concerned with one form of self-deception which is present, Cecilia's having fooled herself until then about her feelings (a concern of Austen's), but rather with another: her certainty at this point that everything will work out perfectly. 'Delighted with so flattering a union of inclination with propriety, she now began to cherish the partiality she at first had repressed, and [thought] the future destination of her life already settled' (IV, ii; II, 144). Cecilia even hopes that Delvile will not immediately declare himself, so that she will have more time to study his character. Burney directs her irony against Cecilia's complacency – 'this happy intellectual arrangement' (IV, iii; II, 146) – and she underlines her point by allowing the complacency to produce some comic misinterpretations of Delvile's behaviour. When Cecilia requests the elder Delvile to reject a suitor whom rumour has made her fiancé, and the younger Delvile reacts with concern at his 'danger' in knowing her free and not engaged, she concludes that he doubts his power to win her affection, an interpretation gratifying to her pride and dignity. Instead, he is determined against loving her, if possible. Cecilia even goes so far as to congratulate herself on Delvile's diffidence, which argues that he is ignorant of her feelings; as a result, she smugly contemplates 'the power of mingling dignity with the frankness with which she meant to receive his addresses' (IV, ix; II, 246). The notion that Cecilia is a paragon and that Burney does not dissociate herself from her, or see her limits, is nonsense, although certainly the irony with which she treats her heroine is clumsy compared to Austen's parallel irony against Elizabeth's pride of judgment, or her treatment in *Emma* of a similar situation: Emma's early complacent delusions about Frank Churchill.

Other elements besides irony in the treatment of Cecilia's character are echoed and then surpassed in *Pride and Prejudice*. Both Cecilia and Delvile are capable of misjudging each other, and in fact are eager to do so even while persuading themselves that they are being candid. Because each feels a need a suppress his affection for the other, each is very ready to think the worst of the other by holding on to certain preconceptions. Delvile, convinced that a woman will always deny an engagement, does not know how to believe Cecilia's denial of the rumour that Sir Robert Floyer has any claim on her; he wants at once to believe and disbelieve it. Both Cecilia and Delvile see candour in each other's manner and fear insincerity hidden beneath the surface. This interaction between feeling and judgment is rather successfully presented in 'A Man of the Ton' (IV, vi), a chapter Austen alludes to in *Persuasion* (189). The interaction is presented, rather than dramatized, and Burney, not the reader, detects self-deception in that 'Cecilia could not refuse [to introduce Delvile to her guardian, Mr Harrel], though as the request was likely to occasion more frequent meetings, she persuaded herself she was unwilling to comply' (IV, vi; II, 198). Nevertheless, the situation Burney contrives is likely to have interested Austen, for here two people of equal intelligence and self-possession are judging each other, not fully aware of their own hearts and thinking themselves safe, indifferent and objective when they are not. Thus, feeling and judgment are at odds, although it must be noted as a vital difference that the tension between them which Burney makes part of her narrative is not made part of the reader's response to the narrative: the reader forms no misconceptions parallel to the characters' own. It is Austen's triumph to control her narrative so that he does. Those tensions between feeling and judgment which Burney does delineate, and the fluxes in feeling which result, are similar in many ways to those which Elizabeth and Darcy undergo at the end of *Pride and Prejudice*. Each is at this point anxious to ascertain the other's feelings and unable to do so, partly because of his own stake in the answer, and partly because mutual embarrassment masks their feelings. Elizabeth's assessments of Darcy's feelings change continually, and all these fluctuations are registered. What differentiates Burney's treatment is that she repeats these effects too much, so that they blur, and this fault undermines her work in general. Austen never similarly confuses repetition with depth or intensity.

The treatment of emotional content offers the most important opportunity to define Austen's interest in and debt to Burney. In *Cecilia*, Austen found an attempt to embody in a non-epistolary novel the themes that concerned her: the conflict between feeling and judgment, and the cost and fluidity of emotional life. Burney's novel has far too much flow and flux, which may have been as useful to Austen as anything else.

One device Burney continually uses was certainly attractive to Austen: that of bringing opposing manners into a comic conjunction not usually thought to possess much emotional resonance. Burney likes to juxtapose vulgarity and good breeding or delicacy, and she arranges that Morrice, Hobson, Simkins, Briggs and of course Mrs Belfield, will all confront and embarrass Cecilia at various times. Mrs Belfield (considered to resemble Mrs Bennet) broadly hints in company that Cecilia loves her son, outrageously and painfully embarrassing both her daughter, Henrietta, and Cecilia; and Cecilia must forbear 'through compassion to the blushing Henrietta . . . repressing this forwardness [of Mrs Belfield] more seriously' (V, ii; III, 40). In such scenes, Burney gives this comic situation thematic content by emphasizing that delicacy and consideration have their costs, and that good breeding is frequently, by its very nature, helpless against the presumption of bad manners and vulgarity. The juxtaposition of different manners is an established formula for comedy, and Burney cannot be credited with its invention. But she does begin to explore its possibilities in narrative fiction by allowing the comic incongruities which result from these juxtapositions to be felt as something more than comic. She can also, unfortunately, go further and allow the difficulties which arise from her heroine's delicacy to become unconvincing and factitious, as they are in Cecilia's 'distress' at the end. Her fate here coincides remarkably with Tompkins' amusing description of the distressed heroine in a hackney-coach, 'with a rising fever and an injured reputation'.[8]

Other aspects of Burney's choice and treatment of emotional content must have interested Austen. Burney shows that pride in combination with other traits results in much complicated and often misplaced or misdirected feeling. When Cecilia fears that Mrs Delvile is about to offer her compassionate assistance in winning Delvile, she resolves 'rather [to] give up Mortimer and all thoughts of him for-ever, than submit to receive assistance in persuading him to the union'; but her fears are wholly groundless, for Mrs Delvile immediately lets her know that she opposes the marriage (VI, viii, III, 313). In Cecilia's initial resolve, however, pride and delicacy cannot be divided, and Burney explores this conjunction throughout. When Cecilia receives Delvile's letter proposing a clandestine marriage, her responses are similarly complex. Comparison between Cecilia's offended pride at Delvile's confession of his scruples and Elizabeth's responses to Darcy's proposal and letter is not quite accurate, for Cecilia is torn between a clandestine marriage and a separation, not between different views of Delvile's character, and Burney is interested in conveying the emotions which make this moral choice impossible for Cecilia. Thus her love for Delvile is alternately combatted by several manifestations of pride, not just by her resentment of his family pride. She is humiliated by suspecting that he proposes the marriage because he feels bound to do so, knowing her love, and consequently she determines to reject him. She also wants to reject him because she fears facing Mrs Delvile's contempt, not simply because of affection for her, but from pride in her good opinion. Later, Cecilia's pride will suggest that she renounce Delvile before Mrs Delvile can ask it (VIII, ii; IV, 195). Vacillations over this choice occupy several chapters, during which false feelings like vanity cannot be disentangled from moral obligations like duty and self-respect (proper pride) or better feelings like love, just as it is impossible to determine whether Cecilia feels that a clandestine marriage is wrong because it is degrading or degrading because it is wrong. The ease with which moral resolves intermingle with and oppose feelings has been established previously at Delvile Castle, where the confusion and pain Cecilia and Delvile experience arise from their eager and conscientious efforts to forestall the pain of a hopeless attachment; all their self-imposed estrangements, and all their attempts to prevent future suffering, are vain, or worse, only increase suffering.

Burney is interested in the emotions which make moral action difficult and in the moral principles which complicate emotions. She shows that reasonable decisions can be made without producing any comfort even in a person who is rational, as exemplified by Cecilia's decision not to go through with the clandestine marriage (VII, vii; IV, 102). Austen is not interested in the classic 'love versus duty' conflict embodied here, however interested she may have been in Burney's portrayal of its emotional costs. In Austen's work the theme of self-knowledge and knowledge of others is substituted, providing all the moral and emotional conflict needed, and providing it more authentically.

The climactic scene of *Cecilia* is the most ambitious in portraying the interaction of feelings and moral obligations, although it is vitiated by stilted diction and other legacies of late eighteenth-century drama. In this scene, Mrs Delvile attempts to persuade Cecilia and her son not to marry, and she does so by appealing to their pride. A conflict results among three different forms of pride and three different sets of obligations. Burney's treatment is effective, for she shows that pride, even when it is admirable (Cecilia's 'pride' is really natural dignity), is much stronger than any sense of duty. Pride is the strongest motive, and all the appeals to duty succeed in exciting pride. The conflict is emotional, though all three characters want to treat it as a conflict of principle requiring moral choice and judgment. Mrs Delvile in particular unscrupulously and relentlessly uses the most powerful emotional weapons available on both Cecilia and Delvile, claiming to appeal to their judgments, but in fact making emotional appeals. For this reason, it is not Cecilia's love for Delvile but rather her relation to Mrs Delvile that forms the novel's emotional centre, both in fact and in intention. Burney indicates this in a letter to Mr Crisp, in which she answers his objections to the scene: 'The conflict scene for Cecilia, between the mother and son, to which you so warmly object, is the very scene for which I wrote the whole book, and so entirely does my plan hang upon it, that I must abide by its reception in the world, or put the whole behind the fire.'[9]

The difficulty for such readers as Mr Crisp lies in dealing with a 'mixed' character like Mrs Delvile. Burney's *Diary and Letters* document the refractoriness of her readers, who desired none but simple and straightforward characters; their preference suggests Austen's own difficulties with and attitudes toward her audience. Another acquaintance of Burney's makes this resistance to complexity clear: ' "But how wonderfully you have contrived," she added, "to make one love Mrs Delvile for her sweetness to Cecilia, notwithstanding all her pride, and always to hope the pride is commanded by the husband.' "[10] Writing again to Mr Crisp, who had similar views, Burney notes:

> The character of Mrs. Delvile struck you in so favourable a light, that you sunk, as I remember I privately noticed to myself, when you mentioned her, all the passages to her disadvantage previous to this conflict, else it would have appeared to you less inconsistent, for the way is paved for it in several places. . . . Your anger at Mrs. Delvile's violence and obduracy are nothing but what I meant to excite; your thinking it unnatural is all that disturbs me.[11]

Burney is attempting to produce in her readers an emotional response of some complexity: to make Mrs Delvile liked, then to show the ugliness which always was present and which her virtues as well as her pride contribute to. Burney feels that her didactic purposes will best be served by creating at least one character whose faults, virtues and pride are thoroughly intermixed, and in doing so (with some success) she does not cater to her audience's demand for simple, unmixed characters. No doubt Mrs Delvile was another of the novel's attractions for Austen, notoriously unsympathetic to unmixed, perfect characters, and even more ambitious than Burney in her design to manipulate her readers' conventional responses to character.

Because the intention and execution of *Cecilia* have been generally underrated, Austen's interest in it has been thought more limited and restricted than it is. *Cecilia* is a flawed novel; nothing has been said here of one of its major flaws, the sentimentality that Burney continually reasserts. Burney wants to indicate that exercise of reason and adherence to principle can produce contentment, or 'self-complacency' as she calls it. Consequently, when Cecilia has decided to forgo the clandestine marriage, Burney wants us to believe that 'she yet found a satisfaction in the sacrifice she had made, that recompensed her for much of her sufferings, and soothed her into something like tranquillity; the true power of virtue she had scarce experienced before' (VII, vii; IV, 104). These assertions of the 'true power of virtue' are merely willed. Burney, willing Cecilia's rational contentment, is consequently forced into the ridiculous position of continually asserting it in spite of all untoward circumstances, and then contriving circumstances yet more untoward to shatter her resolutions and contentment, and move the plot.

Nevertheless, *Cecilia* remains an interesting novel with a respectable structure, some astute observations of emotional life and some engaging treatment of character, especially the character of Mrs Delvile. Burney's achievement with Mrs Delvile, and her readers' documented unwillingness to accept that achievement, provide one of the more important and illuminating links with Austen's intentions and greater achievements, and show the difficulties encountered by those novelists before Austen who tried, like her, to educate their readers' responses rather than to exploit them. A reader evidently prefers to be exploited.

2. *SIR CHARLES GRANDISON*

Burney's attempts and achievements are remote from Austen's in comparison to those of Richardson, especially in *Sir Charles Grandison*, a novel which provides us with parallels in method: in treatment of character and of the reader's response. Austen has long been known as an admirer of Richardson and especially of *Grandison*. Henry Austen, her brother and the author of the 'Biographical Notice' which prefaced the posthumous publication in late 1817 of *Northanger Abbey* and *Persuasion*, notes in his own rather prolix style that 'Richardson's power of creating, and preserving the consistency of his characters, as particularly exemplified in ''Sir Charles Grandison,'' gratified the natural discrimination of her mind, whilst her taste secured her from the errors of his prolix style and tedious narrative' (*NA*, p. 7). Her nephew, J.E.

Austen-Leigh, writing more than fifty years later, is more circumstantial:

> Her knowledge of Richardson's works was such as no one is likely again to acquire, now that the multitude and the merits of our light literature have called off the attention of readers from that great master. Every circumstance narrated in Sir Charles Grandison, all that was ever said or done in the cedar parlour, was familiar to her; and the wedding days of Lady L. and Lady G. were as well remembered as if they had been living friends.[12]

The explicit references to *Grandison* in *Northanger Abbey* (41-2) and in Austen's letters and manuscripts, particularly 'Sir Charles Grandison' (the recently-published play based on the novel), supply further proof of her intimacy with and affection for it. But, more surprisingly, *Grandison* has been generally overlooked in studies of her work. Few modern admirers or even readers of this novel exist, and any other explanation for its neglect, even by students of Richardson, may be unnecessary.

The plot of *Grandison* does not, at first, reveal links with *Pride and Prejudice*. The heroine, Harriet Byron, is a handsome, clever, moderately rich and rather vain orphan of twenty, who is surrounded by doting relatives and friends, and pursued by several suitors. She visits London at the start of the novel, meets a rake, Sir Hargrave Pollexfen, rejects his proposals, is abducted by him, and is finally rescued by the perfect hero, Sir Charles Grandison. She becomes intimate with his sisters, Lady L and Charlotte, and she falls in love with him. His sentiments remain obscure, and eventually his entanglement with an Italian, Lady Clementina della Porretta, is disclosed to Harriet. He considers himself engaged to Clementina and not free to address anyone else, although when he left Italy, more than a year before the novel opens, her family had refused consent to the marriage because he would not become a Catholic. Lady Clementina herself, unable to reconcile her love for a heretic with her religion, had succumbed to madness. The family at last recalls Sir Charles to Italy, hoping that this will cure her. At this point, an account of Sir Charles's previous relations with Clementina, taken from letters he wrote at the time, interrupts the story and elaborates the bare outline of his disclosure to Harriet. Sir Charles then goes to Italy. Clementina is cured, rejects him at last because he will not convert, and encourages him to marry; he returns to England and is immediately accepted by Harriet. A wedding and some further complications with Clementina follow.

In spite of this evident lack of broad parallels between the plots of the novels, narrower ones can be found. For example, when Sir Hargrave proposes marriage to Harriet, we encounter a spirited woman and a suitor who is incredulous at being rejected and whose pride is outraged by it. Sir Hargrave boasts of his consequence and assures Harriet that he likes her 'friends', that is, her connections. He is consequential, like Darcy – and, like him also, sure of success. Harriet, unlike Elizabeth, offers the conventional thanks for his 'good opinion', but when Sir Hargrave asks her to give reasons for rejecting him, she is unconventionally impolite: 'You do not, hesitated I – hit my fancy – Pardon me, Sir'.[13] Like Darcy, Sir Hargrave accuses her of pride and thereby exposes his own. A somewhat less obvious parallel between the novels is to be found in the rebuke Richardson very explicitly contrives for Harriet (the lady who rejects all her suitors finally loves someone out of reach), and the one Austen contrives for Elizabeth's critical judgment (Elizabeth makes wrong judgments throughout). It is worth remembering, however, that the heroine of *Cecilia* encounters a similar rebuke for her smug certainty about her marriage with Delvile. Finally, the subjects debated in *Grandison* reappear in *Pride and Prejudice*: love at first sight is compared to love founded on esteem or merit; marriages of convenience are compared to love matches; and there is even in both a Charlotte who is the heroine's good friend, who endorses marriages of convenience, who debates their advantages with the heroine and who marries a man of inferior talents. Many of these debates appear, however, in *Cecilia*. Resemblances of this sort result from acceptance of standard novelistic material.

The most significant connection between *Pride and Prejudice* and *Grandison* lies in their common concern with the accuracy and persistence of first impressions (or 'first Prejudices' as Richardson has called them [*SL*, p. 252]). In both novels, first impressions are formed, compared, evaluated, and revised, so that the characters' responses to each other are a major part of the action and a clear, well-established thematic concern. Less obviously, concern with first impressions is in both works technical as well as thematic, and here Richardson's major influence upon Austen can be located. The difficulties the characters undergo in estimating each other are also experienced, to some extent, by each reader as he is introduced to, responds to and estimates the characters. The reader is asked to overcome his own first impressions, to conquer his own prejudices and to refine his own perceptions, as he reads of characters who succeed or fail to do precisely these things. Eliciting and controlling the reader's response is a major technical problem for each author. While there are wide differences between Austen's solution of the problem and

Richardson's, clearly his intentions and achievements indicated to her some of the possibilities of the novel.

Richardson's attitude to his readers can be more readily determined than Austen's for he has typically left letters explaining his designs in great detail. His failure to execute these designs completely must be acknowledged; these failures are far easier to register than his successes. Great discrepancies often exist between his avowed intentions and his execution, most notably in *Pamela* but actually in all his novels, even *Clarissa*, and in *Grandison* the discrepancies are glaring. He intends in *Grandison* to interest the reader in favour of Harriet Byron, a paragon with charm, and then to introduce the pathetic Clementina as a rival, so that the reader, Harriet and Sir Charles himself are placed in a dilemma, in one of those 'delicate Situations' so dear to the eighteenth-century moral sense (*SL*, p. 234). Harriet's attempt to do justice to Clementina's claims and to prefer Clementina's happiness with Sir Charles to her own is thus meant by Richardson to be paralleled by a similar struggle on the reader's part. To Lady Bradshaigh, a favourite correspondent who is reading the novel-in-progress, Richardson exults:

And are you Madam, over Head and Ears in Love, and even with those you once hated? I knew you would – For is not the *Witch* [Clementina] an Honour to her Sex by her Magnanimity; while Harriet excells in all the gentle, the lenient, let me say, the Characteristic Qualities of an amiable Woman? – In many Instances of this Piece, I have, designedly, play'd the Rogue with my Readers; intending to make them think now one way, now another, of the very same Characters. . . . Did I not give you Warning how you suffered your Indignation to rise against Clementina? I knew you would admire her, and pity her and Harriet by Turns. My Hero only, I hoped, you would always think of in one Way (*SL*, p. 248).

His intentions are made even more explicit in a subsequent letter:

So far as you had gone Oct. 31 Clementina appears to have the Advantage of Harriet; Why then quarrelled your Ladiship with one of your Favourite Hearers, for thinking so? Let me have the Pleasure I hoped for, of turning my Readers Hearts now one way, now another. My Compliments to this good Lady, I pray ye, Madam, who can divest herself of first Prejudices, and, like Sir Charles, prefer according to Merit, as that Merit shines dazlingly forth (*SL*, p. 252).

This rivalry between the moral merits of Clementina and Harriet is to modern taste one of the novel's least successful elements. Harriet's willingness to renounce her own happiness in favour of Clementina's seems either ridiculous or merely neurotic by modern standards, but certainly not noble. Clementina's renunciation of temporal bliss with Sir Charles to avoid endangering her eternal bliss is so 'elevated', so 'exalted', so 'soaring', that indeed it rises above emotional conflict and moral choice altogether: who would not, given the certainty of either, prefer eternal to temporal bliss? At the same time, one or two modern readers are interested enough in the characters of Harriet and Clementina to compare and choose between them – and actually choose Clementina. E. A. Baker is the most adamant, declaring Harriet 'of no significance as a person,' while Clementina 'is so much more impressive than the generality of [Richardson's] characters.'[14] In fact, she is less impressive; she is melodramatic. Her madness, for example, is merely theatrical, expressed in the stilted diction and gestures of melodrama. Richardson is, however, willing to show petulance and hostility in Clementina when she is sane, and any vitality or interest she has arises from her irritable fears and perceptions that Sir Charles fails to respond to her, to meet her feelings or to love her. Irritability is always Richardson's forte, but he does not allow Clementina enough of this or any other emotional complexity to save her from being a construct, not a character.

This is even more true of Sir Charles, who is only to be thought of 'one way'. Richardson's 'good man' is intentionally excluded from the novel's concern with manipulating impressions, and any other life he might have had is driven out by his exemplary nature: Sir Charles is not a good but a perfect man, and thus he is finally unmanageable. Austen at fifteen proved herself a most astute critic of Sir Charles's absurd perfection when she wrote her hilarious spoof, 'Jack and Alice'. Its first chapters in particular constitute a sustained and even explicit parody of the novel; one character, 'like the great Sir Charles Grandison scorned to deny herself when at Home, as she looked on that fashionable method of shutting out disagreable Visitors, as little less than downright Bigamy' (*MW*, p. 15). This joke on the hero's near-bigamous situation is only slightly less penetrating than the sustained burlesque provided in the character of Charles Adams. The youthful Austen hits off just what is ridiculous in Richardson's treatment of Sir Charles (whose 'dazzling' merit too often suggests celestial objects to his admirers) when she introduces Charles Adams as 'an amiable, accomplished & bewitching young Man; of so dazzling a Beauty that none but Eagles could look him in the Face' and continues by portraying him at a masquerade:

Of the Males a Mask representing the Sun, was the most universally admired. The Beams that darted from his Eyes were like those of that glorious Luminary tho' infinitely superior. So strong were they that no one dared venture within half a mile of them. . . . The Gentleman at last finding the feirceness of his beams to be very inconvenient to the concourse by obliging them to croud together in one corner of the room, half shut his eyes by which means, the Company discovered him to be Charles Adams in his plain green Coat, without any mask at all (*MW*, p. 13).

A last comment on Sir Charles is supplied when Charles Adams, pursued by several ladies, remarks, 'I expect nothing more in my wife than my wife will find in me – Perfection' (*MW*, p. 26). Austen's mature response to *Grandison* is contained in *Emma*. In both novels, a perfect hero marries a lively, witty, vain and faulty heroine instead of a more serious and reserved foil (Jane Fairfax, Clementina) who suffers in mind and body from an enforced concealment of love. The parallelism is imperfect. Nevertheless, Austen's power to create a character as full of perfection as Sir Charles but, unlike him, vivid, vigorous, charming and sexually attractive, is unique, and becomes most obvious when compared to Richardson's failure.

Richardson indirectly acknowledges his difficulties when he writes that *Grandison* 'is said to abound with delicate Situations. I hope it does; for what indelicate ones can a good Man be involved in? – Yet he must have his Trials, his Perplexities – And to have them from good Women, will require some Management' (*SL*, p. 234). The difficulty is that Sir Charles's feelings must be as irreproachable as his actions. There can never be any doubt that his feelings, whatever they may be, will be as well-regulated by his honour and judgment as is his conduct. Thus, his sufferings in Italy over Clementina, however carefully described, cannot really be taken seriously and can be felt only as embarrassment, not as conflict: Sir Charles will so soon be feeling the right, the exemplary, thing. Richardson does, however, succeed in providing another dimension for Sir Charles's feelings which excites some interest: mysteriousness. Like the characters, the reader is forced to guess at what Sir Charles feels for Harriet and Clementina at various points, and to this extent, his imagination is engaged, his judgment is at stake, and he turns 'now one way, now another' in his view of what those feelings are, even though he can be sure of their purity and that their cost to Sir Charles will in the end be minimal.

An important question remains, however: how much does Sir Charles himself share this perplexity over the state of his own heart? Do his ambiguous accounts of his feelings indicate that his judgment, self-knowledge and conduct are subject in any way to the errors the other characters show? Every Richardsonian character is his own apologist, and Richardson, no mean apologist on his own behalf, draws his power as a novelist partially from this source. His strength lies in his ability to involve himself imaginatively in his characters' attempts at self-justification and, at the same time, to dissociate himself enough to indicate the delusions, vanities and egoism behind them. *Grandison* harnesses this strength and this material for its comic and didactic purposes. All the characters are clearly intended to be fallible judges of themselves and others – except Sir Charles. Richardson's eagerness to display constant disinterestedness in Sir Charles conflicts with his reluctance to offer either Harriet or Clementina the indignity of being loved less than she loves. These opposite claims force Richardson to place Sir Charles in the incongruous position of claiming to be disinterested in relation to Clementina when he is, at least in part, uninterested, and nowhere in the novel is this incongruity recognized. Clearly, it is not to be felt as incongruous. While the reader is rewarded for attentiveness to similar discrepancies and contradictions in the motives of the other characters, he is discouraged from such scrutiny of Sir Charles.

Accordingly, the sixth volume, containing the courtship of Harriet, is less effective than it might have been, for only Harriet's feelings invite examination. That they do is a welcome change, however, for Harriet has been in lovesick eclipse since she first learned of Sir Charles's entanglement, two volumes and a half before. Her situation, or 'love case', offers Richardson opportunities to contrive scenes increasingly complicated with embarrassments and reticence, or with cross-currents of feeling and awareness. Through these, as Alan D. McKillop notes, '*Grandison* showed the way to the substitution of social embarrassment for tragic conflict, to a light transcription of manners, and to a "delicacy" which was sometimes silly but at its best penetrating and subtle' and the novel, thereby, 'established the tradition in which Jane Austen triumphed'.[15] In one scene which Austen must have relished, Sir Charles confers with his sisters, Lord L. and Harriet on Charlotte Grandison's love case (her entanglement with Captain Anderson, an unworthy suitor) before Harriet has confessed her love to the sisters but not before they suspect it. Sir Charles moralizes from Charlotte's unfortunate experience:

> Let me repeat, that women should be *sure* of their men, before they embark with them in the voyage of Love. . . . Let me say, That women,

who would not be *exposed*, should not put themselves out of their own power. O Miss Byron! (turning, to my confusion, to me, who was too ready to apply the first part of the caution) be so good as to tell my Emily, that she never love a man, of whose Love she is not well assured: That she never permit a man to know his consequence with her, 'till she is sure he is grateful, just, and generous' (II, xxix; I, 412).

The ironic effect of this passage is not only immediate (Harriet is not 'sure' of her man), but also linear. Emily, Sir Charles's fourteen-year-old ward, is later discovered to be in love with Sir Charles without knowing it herself. The incident also serves the action, although indirectly: Charlotte's embarrassment at her exposure in this scene prompts her in the text to tease Harriet into revealing her love. Once Harriet's love is known to Charlotte and Lord and Lady L, more complex effects are possible. One fine scene collects the same participants and depicts Sir Charles, just prior to his disclosure to Harriet of his own love case, enquiring of his sister Charlotte whether she will encourage Lord G's addresses. Charlotte is conventionally coy about her feelings and Sir Charles criticizes her flippancy, comparing her unfavourably with Harriet, whom he commends for her frankness to her suitors about the state of her heart. But Harriet cannot frankly own her love for Sir Charles and finds herself in a false position, becoming increasingly embarrassed by every sentence in Sir Charles's and Charlotte's exchange.

Soon after this scene, Sir Charles does disclose to Harriet his situation with Clementina; most unfortunately, for thereafter Richardson finds it impossible to treat Harriet with irony. Hitherto, he has contrived not merely to embarrass but also to chasten Harriet, in the first place, by allowing her comfortable indifference to her suitors to be succeeded by love for a man who does not court her. Similarly, Harriet's preconception (or 'prejudice') in favour of being someone's first love, and her idea that only thus can she expect truly gratifying and tender sentiments, is utterly defeated by Sir Charles's situation. In the end, she accepts him in defiance not only of this prejudice but of decorum as well, and her petulance, fears and jealousies at finding herself in this position revive interest in her as a character, after her decline (in every sense) while Clementina's story is pursued. Nevertheless, thanks to Sir Charles's perfections, Harriet's doubts and fears and withdrawals during his courtship, which would be quite justifiable in relation to any other man in similar circumstances, here look like conventional virgin modesty carried to an utterly ridiculous extreme. Richardson's contemporaries found it so. The bluestocking Elizabeth Carter wrote to Catherine Talbot, one of Richardson's consultants on *Grandison*, that 'The courtship between Sir Charles and Miss Byron is very much laughed at, even by those who are best pleased with the book'.[16] Richardson's knowledge of the human heart and his talent for dramatizing its conflicts are undermined by the inhumanly irreproachable heart of Sir Charles.

Charlotte's love case, a conventional one, is more interesting than that of Sir Charles, Clementina or Harriet: should a woman of 'superior talents' marry a man inferior to her? Her dilemma suggests that of her namesake in *Pride and Prejudice* in some ways, although Charlotte Lucas is cursed by plainness and poverty as Charlotte Grandison is not, and Mr Collins is far more objectionable than Lord G. Both Richardson and Austen use this dilemma to engage the reader's judgment of each marriage along with the characters', and both novelists arrange that these judgments will be revaluated several times. In fact, in his treatment of Charlotte Grandison, Richardson manipulates first impressions of character and circumstance in a manner that most closely approaches Austen's.

Charlotte does marry Lord G, and the reader's interest in this marriage is obtained in defiance of Richardson's own complaint to one of his correspondents that 'you girls generally care not a farthing for the story of an honest couple after the knot is tied' (*SL*, p. 187). Richardson manages this by making Charlotte's character the most interesting and appealing one in the novel. He succeeds in controlling his readers' impressions, making them think 'now one way, now another' of her, though certainly not always precisely according to his intention:

> For Instance – Did not you like Charlotte, at her first Appearance? Did you not afterwards in the Affair of Capt. Anderson despise her? Did you not abhor her for her Insolence to Harriet in her Dressing-Room? and still more for her Behaviour to her Lord (done, perhaps, to make less flippant Wives, tho' flippant enough, tolerable to their Husbands)? I know you did – But take Care, that you are not at last diverted wth. that very Humour, for which now you detest her (*SL*, p. 248).

In the first half of the novel, Richardson does elicit from the reader complex and vacillating feelings for Charlotte; in the rest, gratitude for her wit, common sense and perverseness as a relief from the noble and elevated solemnity of the others outweighs everything else.

In his attempt to manipulate his readers' responses, Richardson borrows some of Lovelace's qualities for Charlotte, and adapts others. Like Lovelace, she sees herself in dramatic roles, and creates comic

confrontations. Like him also, she is extremely sensitive to and comfortable with sexual innuendo, using it as a weapon against more
conventional characters – often to attack conventional demands that she
be a submissive wife. When her sister and Harriet try to persuade
Charlotte to give a wedding present of a thousand pounds to her
husband, she responds,

> wot ye not the indelicacy of an *early* present, which you are not *obliged*
> to make? We were both silent, each expecting the other to answer the
> strange creature. She laughed at us both. Soft souls, and tender! said
> she, let me tell you, that there is more indelicacy in delicacy, than you
> *very* delicate people are aware of (IV, xvii; II, 350).

Her sister's reply shows that Richardson is conscious of the resemblance
to Lovelace: 'Had you been a man, you would have been a sad rake.'
Charlotte's wit, in fact, links her most firmly with Lovelace, and
Richardson's use of both characters' wit to control readers' responses
brings his techniques closest to Austen's in *Pride and Prejudice*. Charlotte's
wit is sometimes a relief from the earnestness of the other characters, and
Richardson, like Austen, can confidently depend upon this favourable
response. At other times, Richardson expects her wit to grate or become
tiresome, as Lovelace's does. Similarly, in her treatment of Mr Bennet and
even of Elizabeth, Austen will exploit the technique of criticizing wit and
making it grate. Charlotte's will is expressed in her wit ('I must have my
jest, I say' [V, xi; II, 509]), and she will not relinquish it. Or rather, she
reforms her behaviour time and again, before and after her marriage, but
outbreaks of orneriness recur as often as she reforms and are both
entertaining and irritating. These outbreaks testify to the vitality,
persistence and pressures of her personality, or of any personality. Her
marriage finally depends more on Lord G's learning to be laughed at by
learning to discriminate between jokes and contempt, than on Charlotte's
learning to discriminate between jokes and petulance.[17] By insisting on
remaining herself while making necessary and gradual but still reluctant
adjustments to the demands and feelings of others, she becomes a credible,
vital and (on the whole) endearing character. All this must have attracted
Austen, and her most endearing quality certainly did: Charlotte is never
morbid over her faults. She never lets self-criticism become self-
indulgence. 'She makes it a rule, she says, to remember nothing that will
vex her' (IV, i; II, 263), and although the carelessness and flippancy which
this principle allows can be irritating, its healthiness and vitality are

refreshing, and anticipate (without the carelessness) Elizabeth Bennet's own 'philosophy', as she calls it: 'Think only of the past as its remembrance gives you pleasure' (369).

The desirability of love matches, and the 'vincibility' of a first love, are continually debated in *Grandison*, not just by Charlotte. The novel is, in fact, structured according to parallels and contrasts in the various 'love cases' as they unfold, and several characters – Sir Charles, Charlotte, Lucy Selby, Emily and perhaps Clementina – are made to overcome a first love by the end of the novel. To do so is not quite to overcome a first impression, however – a subject fully exploited by Austen. Although first impressions are frequently registered in *Grandison*, their formation and persistence are not debated at any length, as they are in *Pride and Prejudice*. This theme appears only in Richardson's attempt to manipulate the reader's responses to the characters. Again, his letters provide statements of the theme and considerable evidence for its importance in his conception of his work. Writing to Lady Bradshaigh, Richardson is most explicit about his designs:

> Harriet, you say, looks *little*. – Now, Madam, am I at the Heighth of my Wishes in the Power you have given me over your Prejudices in favour of her. – Take care, that your Convictions have their proper Force; and do not permit your Prejudices to recurr, unless you find a Merit superior to that of Clementina, arise for the now diminished Harriet. Very seldom have I found Ladies, tho' temporarily convinced, act up to their Acknowledgements, against a declared first Opinion (*SL*, p. 254).

In this case, Richardson wants the 'first Opinion' to recur, and Harriet to supplant Clementina; he is enjoying in advance the further power over her prejudices which he promises himself. He is not disappointed, and he later writes complimenting Lady Bradshaigh's head and heart at the expense of the common reader's:

> Ye World is not enough used to this way of writing, to the moment. It knows not that in the minutiae lie often the unfoldings of the Story, as well as of the heart; & judges of an action undecided, as if it were absolutely decided. Nor will it easily part wth. its first impressions. How few Lady B's who will read it over once for Amusement, and a second time to examine into the unjustness or justness of its several parts, as they contribute to make one Whole! (*SL*, p. 289).

Finally: 'We often cheat ourselves on the Entrance into a Character, by setting it down in our minds for such or such and when it rises or sinks upon us, are hardly able to reconcile it to our first hasty Impressions. And who is it that is not fond of justifying his first impressions, in compliment to himself?' (*SL*, pp. 287–8). This statement provides almost a formula for the process Austen intends to elicit and to correct in the readers of *Pride and Prejudice*, at the same time as she presents and corrects it in Elizabeth.

Pride and Prejudice embodies, then, Richardson's intention to manipulate and educate the reader's first impressions of character. The question of 'first impressions' is actually debated in *Pride and Prejudice*, unlike *Grandison*, by the central characters; this is one of the most important differences between the novels, and one which contributes to the superiority of *Pride and Prejudice*. It is the first of Austen's novels in which the difficulty of judgment and of response is treated by the characters themselves as a central issue. This issue is not, unfortunately, treated by Austen in *her* correspondence, although her letters are full of jokes about first impressions of new acquaintances. Richardson's correspondence, however suggestive, is limited in its usefulness: statements of his intentions cannot be evidence for his achievements, and are not evidence of what Austen learned from *Grandison*. Yet Richardson does to some extent achieve his intentions in the novel, though not with the brilliance and subtlety that he does in *Clarissa*. *Sir Charles Grandison* clearly represents an attempt to combat inattention and misjudgment in his readers and to develop their capacities for sensitive and candid judgments. Sir Charles pronounces a kind of moral or motto for the novel when he says, 'No one can judge of another, that cannot be that very other in imagination, when he takes the judgment-seat' (II, xx; I, 365). Richardson's attempts to harness his incorrigible readers, however, and to induce them to give him power over their prejudices often become harassment. Austen does not fuss over her readers' responses, however she may hope to direct them, nor does she judge her readers by their responses, as Richardson certainly does: 'it is inconceivable how much advantage, in my proud heart, is given me, of peeping into the hearts of my readers, and sometimes into their heads, by their approbation, and disapprobation, of the conduct of the different persons in my Drama' (*SL*, p. 289). 'But a great deal in charity to them,' he goes on to say, 'I attribute to their inattention,' resuming his candour although relinquishing none of his demands.

Austen is more detached, and in fact compiled diverse 'Opinions' of *Mansfield Park* and *Emma*, clearly delighting in their incongruities, idiosyncrasies and inconsequence. A sample, on *Mansfield Park*, nicely illustrates these qualities:

> Miss Burrell – admired it very much – particularly Mrs Norris & Dr Grant. –
>
> Mrs Bramstone – much pleased with it; particularly with the character of Fanny, as being so very natural. Thought Lady Bertram like herself. – Preferred it to either of the others – but imagined *that* might be her want of Taste – as she does not understand Wit. –
>
> Mrs Augusta Bramstone – owned that she thought S & S. – and P. & P. downright nonsense, but expected to like M P. better, & having finished the 1st vol. – flattered herself she had got through the worst.
>
> The families at Deane – all pleased with it. – Mrs Anna Harwood delighted with Mrs Norris & the green curtain (*MW*, p. 433).

The 'Opinions' show that Austen recognizes and is interested in the problem of readers' responses, however different her own attitude is from Richardson's. As a very careful and enthusiastic student of *Grandison*, she probably came as close to the novel's ideal reader as possible. She may have learned from Richardson to consider manipulation of the reader's response as the first goal of fiction and as the major problem it faces. Clearly, she considers such manipulation an opportunity not to be missed. Her debt to Richardson's intentions in *Grandison* – to educate his readers' responses through a series of 'love cases' in a comic novel – cannot be defined more precisely; she could have found these aims, in this form, nowhere else, and it is immaterial whether she borrowed them consciously or simply found them congenial.

If Richardson's themes and intentions are congenial, are his methods and techniques equally so? Both authors required devices to manipulate their readers' judgments and sympathies; both had to find or create novelistic conventions to convey the confusions and obliquities of feeling and of social life. Austen, however, rejects the epistolary form with which Richardson is able to reproduce events not yet clear or patterned, and with which he records flux of feeling, as far as each character understands it. The form demands great attention from readers and taxes their memories. Austen finds different methods that tax her readers quite as thoroughly – dialogue, for example. Richardson notoriously stretches his form to include long sections of dialogue, often among several characters, and Austen must have learned much from his ability to portray in ordinary polite conversation the contending personalities and some of the conflicting feelings of a small group of characters, although her dialogue is far more economical than Richardson's, as well as more playful and entertaining. By the time she writes *Pride and Prejudice*, Austen finds in dialogue a means to register fluctuations in feeling, and in the wit and charm of her characters a means to control readers' responses. In the earlier works dialogue, where it exists, is either superficially 'characteristic' or simply comic, and she relies on other devices to direct the reader's response. But in *Pride and Prejudice*, and even more strikingly in *Emma*, she succeeds in making wit both endearing and irritating, as Richardson does. His attitude toward wit is more ambivalent than Austen's, so his eagerness in *Grandison* to criticize it is not surprising. More surprising is his interest in registering the costs of the very virtues he most wishes to encourage in his readers, frankness and impartiality. Harriet Byron's frankness means that everyone knows of her hopeless love for Sir Charles, with resulting embarrassment for her; and Sir Charles's fair, impartial judgment encourages other characters to demand unselfishness from him, and to make no allowances for his feelings. This is the price of perfection in a character, and the reader too is disinclined to allow for Sir Charles's feelings. In *Pride and Prejudice*, the ironic treatment of frankness and of judgment is both more subtle and more sustained, yet Austen's works do share with Richardson's a concern to render the difficulties inherent in exercising those qualities which obtain their approval.

Other effects and structures in *Grandison* reappear in *Pride and Prejudice*, modified to suit a non-epistolary novel. Unorganized experience, which the epistolary form intrinsically registers, is conveyed in *Pride and Prejudice* by anticlimax: the ebb and flow of expectation and disappointment, especially over the early romances between Jane and Bingley and Elizabeth and Wickham. The technique of violating or playing with the reader's conventional novelistic expectations, a technique based upon an acute awareness and distrust of the stock responses which these expectations permit when not interfered with, is not an exclusive property of Richardson or Austen. The device is present in Burney's novels, among others; but in the works of Richardson and Austen it becomes an important means with which to manipulate the reader, forcing him to accept complexity of feeling, not simplicity or a stock response. In this way, the reader is made to accept Elizabeth's reaction to seeing Pemberley for the first time (her very unconventional feeling that 'to be mistress of Pemberley might be something' [245]), and to accept Harriet Byron's partially unrequited love. The advantage of this technique lies in its obviousness: the reader is conscious that he is being challenged, and the narrator or characters will often discuss the difficulty openly. The final technical device which Richardson and Austen share, the use of parallels and contrasts to enlarge the scope of the action and to guide the reader's interpretation of it, is shared also by most writers of narrative. In *Grandison* as in *Pride and Prejudice* and so many other works, characters and marriages are contrasted and used as foils to one another. This time-worn literary device, so essential to *Pride and Prejudice*, raises problems of a particular sort in evaluating that novel.

4 Pride and Prejudice

Pride and Prejudice (1813) is perhaps the most difficult of Austen's works, partly because it is so popular and so memorable. For some readers it is the first and most often read of the six novels, and for most its plot is so vivid and definite that it is unforgettable. This creates a special problem: the text is likely to be over-familiar, making a fresh or even an attentive response difficult. For example, modern critics are unanimous in claiming that the novel tends toward union of opposites,[1] toward a kind of wholeness and perfection. Yet a close examination of the first six chapters reveals surprising discontinuities, beginning with an unusual delay in presenting the themes implied by the title (only in *Persuasion* does Austen similarly defer this presentation). The first four chapters deal with the problem of 'first impressions', reminding us of *Grandison*. Chapters I and II are well-known for their entertaining exchanges exposing Mrs Bennet's foolishness and Mr Bennet's wit. These characters expose themselves by dwelling not simply on the subject of marriage but also on the conventions which control social introductions, a subject kept in view for some time. Mr Bennet takes an anti-conventional stance in the first chapter; when his wife insists that 'Indeed you must go, for it will be impossible for *us* to visit him, if you do not,' he replies, making fun of this confusion of an introduction with a marriage: 'You are over scrupulous surely. I dare say Mr Bingley will be very glad to see you; and I will send a few lines by you to assure him of my hearty consent to his marrying which ever he chuses of the girls' (4). In the next chapter he reverses himself by mock approval of the conventions, and he plays on the discrepancy between knowing someone socially and knowing him indeed, by deliberately misinterpreting his wife's 'I am not acquainted with him myself': 'I honour your circumspection. A fortnight's acquaintance is certainly very little. One cannot know what a man really is by the end of a fortnight' (7). It is all entertaining and reveals Mr and Mrs Bennet for us, but it all seems to belong in a book called *First Impressions* rather than *Pride and Prejudice*.

The incidents of the next two chapters continue this emphasis on introductions. The subject of pride is not completely submerged in this exposition, but Darcy's pride seems described only to be linked to its various

87

effects on people's judgments of him, a 'first impressions' emphasis. Even
the most shocking demonstration of his pride, his insulting refusal to
dance with Elizabeth, provides opportunities for judgments, particularly
in Chapter V, where for the first time 'pride' as a theme receives
consideration. The chapter begins with a description of the caricature, Sir
William Lucas, who combines pride and affability just as Darcy combines
pride and incivility, or as Mr Collins later will combine pride and
servility; and in the very next chapter Sir William and Darcy are made to
confront each other on the subject of dancing, so that the opposition
between them becomes unmistakable, and comic as well. Sir William
reminds us of a novel like *Cecilia*, and the fifth chapter as a whole reminds
us of the moral debates inserted in eighteenth-century novels. A good
example of these debates is supplied by the second chapter of *Cecilia*, titled
'An Argument.' Genius and its obligation either to comply with or to
defy convention is discussed by the two opposed characters Belfield and
Monckton. In *Pride and Prejudice*, the 'debate' is treated humorously, and
we hear the vulgar voice of Mrs Bennet, the candid voice of Jane, the
worldly and practical voice of Charlotte, the moralizing voice of Mary,
and the ironic voice of Elizabeth discoursing on the subject of pride, a
discourse which descends abruptly to an idiotic argument between Mrs
Bennet and a 'young Lucas'. This descent serves equally to undercut
literary debates of this sort and to round off the chapter. Thus, although
'pride' has now been brought forward, it has been treated in a very
cavalier manner.

This delay or indirection in presenting the themes announced by the
title is paralleled by other assaults on the reader's expectations. Bingley
seems to be the hero until Chapter VI, when Darcy's interest in Elizabeth
is discovered. Elizabeth's own importance is not perfectly clear
until Chapter IV, after Darcy's insult, when she discusses the ball with
Jane. And the 'fixed' characters, Mr and Mrs Bennet, who are presented
in the first chapter complete with capsule descriptions, mislead the reader
into thinking 'character' will be a predictable and reliable quality in the
novel, as readily ascertained as in *Sense and Sensibility*. There are even
traces of Austen's earlier burlesque manner.

As if all these elements were not enough for the reader to assimilate,
Austen includes in her first few chapters some further superficial but still
surprising parallels to the opening chapters of *Cecilia*. Comprehensive
summaries of character, common in Burney's novels, are less so in
Austen's, but the familiar summary of Mrs Bennet's character at the end
of Chapter I – '*Her* mind was less difficult to develope. She was a woman
of mean understanding, little information, and uncertain temper. When

she was discontented she fancied herself nervous. The business of her life was to get her daughters married; its solace was visiting and news' (5) – is quite like the summary at the start of Chapter II in *Cecilia* of the character of Lady Margaret Monckton's companion, actually named Miss Bennet: 'she was low-born, meanly educated, and narrow-minded; a stranger alike to innate merit or acquired accomplishments, yet skilful in the art of flattery, and an adept in every species of low cunning. [She had] no other view in life than the attainment of affluence without labour' (I, ii; I, 14). This resemblance is probably coincidental, and if not, is probably intended to mock Burney's inclusion of characters like Miss Bennet who scarcely reappear and who are 'introduced', as Austen remarks, in a letter criticizing another author's characters, 'apparently merely to be delineated' (*L*, p. 32). A more difficult parallel exists between a passage in *Cecilia* and the famous opening lines of *Pride and Prejudice*: 'It is a truth universally acknowledged, that a single man in possession of a good fortune, must be in want of a wife. However little known the feelings or views of such a man may be on his first entering a neighbourhood, this truth is so well fixed in the minds of the surrounding families, that he is considered as the rightful property of some one or other of their daughters' (3). Because Cecilia is an heiress, she takes Bingley's place in the above formula and is revealed in the first chapter as the intended prey of Mr Monckton, a major force in the plot, who 'had long looked upon her as his future property; as such . . . he had already appropriated her estate' (I, i; I, 11).

If these two passages were less prominent, and if they had less relation to the succeeding action, their similar motif could be dismissed quite easily, since Austen's brilliant style and tone clearly owe nothing to Burney. As it is, the resemblance is puzzling, and typical of the difficulties presented by the first chapters of *Pride and Prejudice*. These difficulties stem from an initial lack of overall focus, which does not result in shapelessness but does dispel unity. The reader focuses upon a succession of sharp, brilliantly defined scenes, characters, descriptions or themes, all equally vivid, and can draw any number of parallels between them (not to mention parallels with other works), but not at the same time. Each scene competes for attention; each is discrete and discontinuous, just as each of the first six chapters is highly structured and sharply defined but is, partly as a result, separable and somewhat isolated from the others. The breaks between the opening chapters are oddly abrupt, and the chapters themselves tend to be very short and clipped, in a manner not elsewhere to be found in the novels.

The initial version of *Pride and Prejudice*, 'First Impressions,' was written between 1796–7. It was reworded extensively, apparently plotted according to the 1811–12 calendar,[2] and published under its present title in 1813. Austen's own comment, that she had 'lop't and crop't so successfully ... that I imagine it must be rather shorter than S. & S. altogether' (*L*, p. 298), suggests extensive cutting. It would be extraordinary if a work with this history were completely unified in its construction, whatever its surface unity or polish. It is more likely to retain abandoned scaffolding and passages which lead nowhere. Accordingly, one might reasonably expect *Pride and Prejudice* to be overworked, over-polished and over-ingenious compared to the other novels; and it is so.

The elaborate and complex connections with *Cecilia* and *Sir Charles Grandison* fully illustrate the extreme ingenuity of *Pride and Prejudice*. Its themes combine the study of pride evident in *Cecilia* with the manipulation of first impressions characteristic of *Grandison*. How far this combination was specifically and consciously calculated by Austen cannot be determined, but the novel does successfully encourage its readers to follow Elizabeth Bennet in forming mistaken first impressions of the characters, in retaining them out of pride, and in finally relinquishing them. Austen intends, evidently, to write a didactic comedy of judgment, a comedy which implicates and educates the reader's critical judgment while relentlessly poking fun at it. The techniques which govern the structure and the comedy of manners in *Pride and Prejudice* more than suffice for the three later novels as well, for technique is only too various and visible in this novel, while the later novels select the most effective techniques and use them with far greater economy and density. For these reasons, the techniques of *Pride and Prejudice* require and repay extensive analysis. They are so mastered as to elicit from the reader an absorption in the world of *Pride and Prejudice* which disregards or transcends any disunities or over-polishing in its composition; for the novel does create a powerful impression of unity, whatever disparate elements it contains.

1. MASTERY OF TECHNIQUE: STRUCTURE

The most obvious techniques are structural: parallels and contrasts order the characters and organize the action; and linear irony creates patterns of reversed or undercut judgments within the action. The highly wrought symmetry of *Pride and Prejudice* has been frequently noticed, but Lascelles first formulated the possible cost:

Exactness of symmetry . . . carries with it one danger. The novelist's subtlety of apprehension may be numbed by this other faculty of his for imposing order on what he apprehends. His apprehension of human relationships, for example, may fail to develop or, if it develops, fail to find due expression because he is impelled to simplify these relationships in his story in the interests of its pattern.[3]

Lascelles does not claim that *Pride and Prejudice* is guilty of these faults, but neither does she fully register the astonishing 'exactness of symmetry' the novel exhibits.

(i) Parallels and contrasts

Lady Catherine de Bourgh is very obviously a foil to Darcy, possessing his pride unalloyed by any wit, either as humour or as intelligence. At several points in the novel, parallels and contrasts between Darcy and Lady Catherine are insisted upon, and have considerable effect on Elizabeth's judgment of both characters, and on our own. No objection can be made to this device, schematic as it is. But Austen pursues the scheme until it seems a mechanical reflex: until parallels appear which are extraneous and do not advance the plot or refine its meaning. When the Gardiners discuss Darcy's civility after being introduced to him at Pemberley, their intelligent praise contains what must be deliberate echoes (though lacking the fulsomeness) of Sir William Lucas's and Mr Collins's characteristic and foolish praise of Lady Catherine's civil invitation to dine at Rosings:

> 'I confess,' said [Mr Collins], 'that I should not have been at all surprised by her Ladyship's asking us on Sunday to drink tea and spend the evening at Rosings. I rather expected, from my knowledge of her affability, that it would happen. But who could have foreseen such an attention as this? Who could have imagined that we should receive an invitation to dine there (an invitation moreover including the whole party) so immediately after your arrival!'
> 'I am the less surprised at what has happened,' replied Sir William, 'from that knowledge of what the manners of the great really are, which my situation in life has allowed me to acquire. About the Court, such instances of elegant breeding are not uncommon' (160).

The Gardiners claim, rather like Mr Collins, that Darcy is 'superior to any thing they had expected'; Mr Gardiner notes: 'I was never more surprised than by his behaviour to us. It was more than civil; it was really attentive; and there was no necessity for such attention. His acquaintance with Elizabeth was very trifling' (257). Like Sir William, Mr Gardiner, though having no similar pride in it, adduces his knowledge of the 'great' in his reading of Darcy and shows also his superiority in good breeding to Sir William: 'But perhaps he may be a little whimsical in his civilities. . . . Your great men often are; and therefore I shall not take him at his word about fishing, as he might change his mind another day, and warn me off his grounds' (258).

Such carefully-wrought parallels and contrasts are not, ultimately, sterile or lifeless, though they are sometimes excessive. They allow Austen to guide the reader's interpretation of the action and of the characters, especially of Elizabeth and Darcy. That is, noting 'pattern' engages the reader's vanity and has even a moral dimension: it necessarily involves estimating and judging characters in relation to one another. Austen can also exploit her elaborate patterns to permit her foils or fixed characters to come to life and to unfold, even if not to change.[4] Mr Bennet, for example, is a fixed character. He does not change in the novel. Throughout, his wit is meant to contrast with Elizabeth's, showing both his own imperception and irresponsibility as a father and the dangers of wit which Elizabeth usually escapes. He strikes his characteristic ironic note even when Lydia elopes. Yet he can unfold. In his conversation with Elizabeth over her engagement to Darcy, he becomes sincere and straightforward, exposing his feelings at last: 'But let me advise you to think better of it. I know your disposition, Lizzy. . . . My child, let me not have the grief of seeing *you* unable to respect your partner in life. You know not what you are about' (376). The poignancy of the final sentences depends on the contrast between the feeling behind them, and Mr Bennet's usual unconcerned, ironic stance, established by so many scenes. Without that reiteration, this scene would have little effect. But as it is, Mr Bennet's appeal to Elizabeth reveals the depth of his love for her, and the reader is nearly as much affected by it as Elizabeth. Austen's mastery of these touches accounts for the reader's absorption in the world of the novel, a world that keeps unfolding, and in which a meticulous structure allows each commonplace incident to acquire resonance from the incidents that precede and follow it.

Although Austen can use her structures to elicit these emotional effects, a sheer delight in pattern for its own sake is also very much in evidence. The contrasts and parallels are indeed frequently carried further than strictly necessary to make thematic points or to reveal character. These overdrawn or superfluous structures are the signature of Austen's early work. She will later subdue them to allow her characters to interact more subtly and, on the whole, more movingly. Yet the patterns in *Pride and Prejudice*, however elaborate, are not in the end mechanical. The reader is, after all, merely exposed to them. Austen does not harass or pursue him with a tag for every point. The reader is left to discover connections for himself, an activity that furthers intimacy with and absorption in the novel while underlining its theme: a comic exploration of complacency or pride of judgment.

(ii) Linear irony

The major structural device in *Pride and Prejudice* is the creation of ironies within the novel's action which, like parallels and contrasts, challenge the reader's attention and judgment throughout, and in the end also engage his feelings. The reversal in Elizabeth's opinion of Darcy which provides the overall, simple structure of the novel also dictates details of structure, but these, the lesser reversals or undercuttings of judgment, are not spelled out as clearly as is the re-estimation of Darcy. Instead, the reader is generally required to perceive them for himself by making appropriate connections between anticipations or judgments and the events which subsequently contradict them. The effects of this linear irony are not immediate, and it is a less satisfying means of challenging or engaging the reader's judgment than the devices Austen finds in the conventions of the comedy of manners. Nevertheless, these reversals do offer a fair means of engaging and testing the reader's sympathies and judgments without actually misleading him. The reader is likely to make the same errors in judgment and feeling that Elizabeth does, but he is not forced to. Austen's techniques for encouraging misjudgments are so effective that a reader dazzled by Elizabeth's charm may overlook some of her lesser mistakes or inaccuracies even in a second or third reading, although these are quite clearly indicated in the text. Whatever success the structure obtains, however, in alternately lulling and exercising the reader's power of judgment, its action does force upon the main characters two kinds of reversals in judgment: first, the characters' expectations and judgments of *other* characters are repeatedly contradicted as the action unfolds; and second, the main characters find themselves forced to contradict or reverse many of their original statements and notions of *themselves*.

The first of these ironies is the most prominent element in the action. Anticipations are quite systematically thwarted or undercut, particularly those which arise from a character's propensity to credit others with his own feelings – even though this propensity (the 'sympathetic imagination', in Lascelles' phrase) is, when purged of mere egoism, one of the qualities the entire novel is designed to exercise and develop. Thus Elizabeth predicts misery for Lydia in her first encounter with Mrs Gardiner after the elopement, and both Jane and Elizabeth dread her homecoming as Mrs Wickham. Of course, they are egregiously in error: 'Lydia was Lydia still; untamed, unabashed, wild, noisy, and fearless' (315). Even Lydia's marriage is not quite as disastrous as Elizabeth anticipates, although her gloomy prognostications for Charlotte's marriage, undercut as they are by Charlotte's 'evident enjoyment' of her lot (157), are both more striking and more amusing. Jane's candour has the advantage here, as in Darcy's case, over Elizabeth's righteous indignation: 'You shall not defend her, though it is Charlotte Lucas. You shall not, for the sake of one individual, change the meaning of principle and integrity, nor endeavour to persuade yourself or me, that selfishness is prudence, and insensibility of danger, security for happiness' (135–6). However admirable this judgment is in principle, it is less adequate to the actual consequences of the marriage than is Jane's mild reply: 'I must think your language too strong in speaking of both . . . and I hope you will be convinced of it, by seeing them happy together' (136). While the Collins menage is certainly not the novel's norm, neither is it the horror that Elizabeth anticipates. Austen will treat Elizabeth's judgment of Charlotte with even stronger linear irony, however. Elizabeth's response at the close of Volume I, 'Engaged to Mr Collins! my dear Charlotte, – impossible!' (124), returns upon her near the end of Volume III when she announces to Jane her own engagement. Jane exclaims, 'You are joking, Lizzy. This cannot be! – engaged to Mr Darcy! No, no you shall not deceive me. I know it to be impossible' (372).

Austen is perfectly conscious that the strong language of Elizabeth's judgments makes them both more noticeable and, in general, more attractive than the characteristic mildness of Jane's. She depends on this kind of response and learns to exploit it thoroughly. The subtle and sensitive judgments which Austen requires her characters and her readers to reach by the end are seldom to be found in Elizabeth at the start. Wilful blindness is at work when she refuses to believe that Charlotte is expressing her real sentiments on marriage in Chapter VI; Elizabeth will not listen to her. There is a coarseness in Charlotte, unperceived at first by Elizabeth, which links her to Mr Collins. The woman who is sure all Elizabeth's dislike of Darcy 'would vanish, if she could suppose him to be in her power' (181) is a suitable Mrs Collins, even though she does not deserve Elizabeth's sweeping condemnation.

Linear ironies are most pervasive in Elizabeth's and Darcy's relations with each other. The gross misjudgments each is capable of (Elizabeth

that Darcy is base, Darcy that Elizabeth is 'expecting [his] addresses'
[369]) are corrected by the proposal scene at Hunsford and by Darcy's
subsequent letter, but other corrections or adjustments for lesser errors
must be supplied by the reader, since neither Austen nor the characters
speak of them. For example, the reader is very ready at first to believe that
Elizabeth is as discerning as she thinks. He soon has an opportunity to
qualify that judgment, however, for Elizabeth cannot see that Darcy is
attracted to her. This is an amiably modest error. Still, it is significant:
Elizabeth's discernment has limits, and the reader is offered every chance
to dissociate himself from her judgments. Elizabeth does realize later that
her judgments of Wickham and Darcy have originated in their responses
to her: 'Pleased with the preference of one, and offended by the neglect of
the other, on the very beginning of our acquaintance, I have courted
prepossession and ignorance, and driven reason away, where either were
concerned' (208). She never realizes that Darcy's neglect so quickly
became attraction; the reader, on the other hand, is left free from the start
to allow her imperception to modify his own perception of the action and
his opinion of Darcy and Elizabeth. Austen's complete control of the
linear irony she creates for *Pride and Prejudice* becomes evident when a
contrasting form of irony is considered: her treatment of Darcy's
unnecessarily scrupulous early behaviour to Elizabeth. He does not
perceive Elizabeth's dislike, and thus deliberately withdraws his
attentions, offering her 'nothing that could elevate her with the hope of
influencing his felicity' (60). The irony here is immediate, not linear.
Darcy's imperceptiveness and vanity are ridiculous and increase the
reader's distance from him. Elizabeth's parallel blindness to Darcy's
admiration, on the other hand, is so amiable in its absence of vanity that
the reader draws closer to her, scarcely registering her mistake, and
therefore becoming more likely to acquiesce in her judgments.

Austen learns in the later novels to elicit from her comedy even greater
complexity of feeling than this, but her mastery in *Pride and Prejudice* is
astonishing enough. Thus, Elizabeth's and Darcy's mistakenly confident
notions about each other's feelings at the start of the novel are succeeded
by the reverse: at the end, they are in suspense about each other's feelings,
and increasingly unable to estimate them. Even then, Elizabeth is doomed
to be always incorrect in anticipating Darcy's feelings and reactions. She
is wrong in her interpretation of his behaviour when she tells him of
Lydia's elopement. She supposes he cannot tolerate being the brother-in-
law of Wickham (326). She mistakenly expects him to respond favourably
to Lady Catherine's intervention. She is, finally, completely unable to
interpret his behaviour to her, his silence and his preoccupation, when he

visits Longbourn after Lydia's marriage. Darcy himself does not escape this sort of irony: his indignation at Lady Catherine's 'unjustifiable endeavours' (381) to separate him from Elizabeth reflects back with perfect parallelism on his earlier intervention between Jane and Bingley.

Mistaken judgments and estimations of others do not exhaust the novel's ironies against pride of judgment. Elizabeth and Darcy are forced to reverse some of their own behaviour and some of their ideas of themselves during the course of the action. The central reversals are obvious: Darcy reforms his manners and Elizabeth learns that she is less discerning than she thought. Other reversals underscore these central ones.

The fault Darcy attributes to himself at first – a resentful temper – is overcome in his relation to Elizabeth, whom he forgives for her misjudgment, for her petulant refusal, and (more remarkably) for her just criticisms of his manners. Elizabeth's case – overcoming the fault of wilful misunderstanding – is not strictly parallel, for she does not at first recognize that she is guilty of this fault. She does, however, find herself acting in defiance of her declaration to Mr Collins that she is not 'one of those young ladies (if such young ladies there are) who are so daring as to risk their happiness on the chance of being asked a second time' (107). A simpler, and more immediate, purely comic reversal of this sort is registered by Elizabeth at the end, when Darcy and Bingley visit Longbourn. Her mother's vulgarity makes her feel at first 'that years of happiness could not make Jane or herself amends, for moments of such painful confusion. . . . Yet the misery, for which years of happiness were to offer no compensation, received soon afterwards material relief, from observing how much the beauty of her sister re-kindled the admiration of her former lover' (337). A more important reversal is contained in Elizabeth's inability for some time at the end to be open about her feelings or her knowledge of Bingley's attachment, with Jane, with her father and of course with Darcy. For the reader and for Elizabeth, whose openness about her feelings is one of her charms, this reserve is especially poignant.

These systematic reversals have one obvious and important result: in *Pride and Prejudice*, Austen is relentless in poking fun at critical judgment. The creation of these linear ironies is only one of her techniques for doing so. The processes by which *all* discriminations are made are treated comically, even subversively. One of Austen's favourite ideas, emphasized in every one of her novels, is that good looks and charm can be depended on to produce a favourable response. Her characters frequently illustrate this process in their responses to each other, and Austen uses their wit, charm, energy and other attractive qualities to manipulate her readers' responses as well. Her characters' responses to each other are easier to analyze, however, than those of her readers. Elizabeth in particular is quite blatantly affected in her high estimation of his virtues by Wickham's good looks, manner and apparent attraction to herself. In their first conversation, Wickham declares that he is prevented from exposing Darcy's baseness to himself by his affectionate remembrance of Darcy's father: 'Elizabeth honoured him for such feelings, and thought him handsomer than ever as he expressed them' (80). Austen's delight in such observations at once carries both her and Elizabeth further: 'Elizabeth was again deep in thought, and after a time exclaimed, "To treat in such a manner, the godson, the friend, the favourite of his father!" – She could have added, "A young man too, like *you*, whose very countenance may vouch for your being amiable" ' (80–1). After this, it can come as no surprise that Elizabeth parts from Wickham for Hunsford, 'convinced, that whether married or single, he must always be her model of the amiable and pleasing' (152); or that later, seeing him again after Darcy's revelations, 'She had even learnt to detect, in the very gentleness which had first delighted her, an affectation and a sameness to disgust and weary' (233).

Wickham is not the only character whose manner and attentions have amusing effects on Elizabeth's judgment. Darcy's initial rudeness assists her to her unfavourable judgment of him, and she is governed by similar considerations in her judgment of the Bingley sisters. Unlike Jane, she does not find them charming: 'with a judgment too unassailed by any attention to herself, she was very little disposed to approve them' (15). She likes them later for their attentions to Jane during her illness, and when these are withdrawn, Elizabeth is 'restored . . . to the enjoyment of all her original dislike' (35). Richardson's observation that everyone retains and justifies his first impressions 'in compliment to himself' (*SL*, p. 288) could hardly be more thoroughly exemplified that it is in Elizabeth.

In poking fun at these impressions and judgments, Austen is showing an amused acquaintance with the human heart and amusing herself at Elizabeth's expense. Misjudgments are treated comically here, though they are to receive very different treatment in *Mansfield Park*. The pure comedy of such brief and typical incidents as Lady Catherine's and Mr Collins's misinterpretation of Darcy's dejection at leaving Rosings (they think him in love with his cousin Anne, whereas he is instead the recently rejected lover of Elizabeth) does not conflict with the more complex but still comic tone of other misinterpretations. The tone remains comic even when rather stringent observations are made. Witness Elizabeth's acknowledgement of the obstacles which human nature places in the way of overcoming first impressions: 'The general prejudice against Mr Darcy is so violent, that it would be the death of half the good people in Meryton, to attempt to place him in an amiable light' (226). The implications of this remark are serious, and reflect upon Elizabeth's own conduct, as she knows perfectly well, but the remark is still fundamentally comic. The structure of *Pride and Prejudice* exposes the unreliable and indeed ludicrous processes which inform judgments of character and which dictate that first impressions will be as erroneous as they are tenacious. But discriminations and judgments are thus undercut only so that Austen can insist at the same time on the inevitability of making them and the obligation to do so. The 'moral certainty' in Austen's novels, which is so welcome and so refreshing to many moderns, rests upon the fullest possible perception of the fallibilities of judgment, its inextricable ties to feeling and the inevitable humbling in consequence.

Austen does believe that feelings and judgment can be made to work more closely together. Her novels are constructed to increase this harmonious interaction, not simply in the response of the main characters, but also in the reader's response. As she clearly shows, feeling, especially self-love, is inextricably linked to judgment, an intellectual and moral activity. Yet Austen engages and exploits, manipulates and educates, more than just her reader's vanity. She achieves this engagement largely through her management of the literary conventions available to her, a management which always includes some adaptation or transformation. The convention which, above all, Austen succeeds in adapting and begins to transform in *Pride and Prejudice* is the comedy of manners, a literary convention used by Richardson and Burney among other novelists, but not fully developed by them.

2. DEVELOPMENT OF TECHNIQUE: THE COMEDY OF MANNERS

The usual definition of the comedy of manners derives from Restoration comedy: 'this form deals with the relations and intrigues of gentlemen and ladies living in a polished and sophisticated society, evokes laughter mainly at the violations of social conventions and decorum, and relies for its effect in great part on the wit and sparkle of the dialogue.'[5] This general definition ignores, as it must, the achievement of the best works in the genre (such as *The Way of the World*) in which true wit and good manners serve to define the characters' worth in the world they inhabit. An analogous use of manners to indicate morals, especially in such actions as Mr Knightley's asking Harriet Smith to dance in *Emma* or, conversely, Emma's rudeness to Miss Bates, is frequently noticed and much admired in Austen's novels, though sometimes with an implication that the device is common or conventional, however extraordinary the handling. But models for these incidents are not to be found in the social comedy of novelists who precede Austen. Even Burney and Richardson treat social comedy or the comedy of manners in a way that illuminates Austen's achievement and her mastery, instead of anticipating it, despite a few exceptions in *Sir Charles Grandison*.

The comedy of manners is a literary convention which depends very much on highly-developed and codified social convention, not simply for its material (the 'manners' of a period), but for its significance: its ability to embody in comic confrontations important differences between characters and distinct evaluations of them ('morals'). The social conventions supporting the literary convention must ideally be serious as well as elaborate. The behaviour dictated by social conventions must invite scrutiny and must reward it, so that description of social conduct can be a reliable index to character. Such description has at the same time another function, and one more usually associated with the comedy of manners: the recording of a particular social milieu. This wider and essentially simpler use of the convention, while important, does not serve to define Austen's differences from her predecessors as clearly as does the other use which the convention permits: the possibility of indicating the grossest and most minute discriminations among characters. For in Austen's novels, as Nardin claims, 'All deviations from [the code of propriety] have a meaning; all reveal something about character'; and her study carefully documents the complex ways that Austen uses 'social behavior' as the 'external manifestation' of a character's 'internal moral and psychological condition'.[6]

(i) Manners

Before Austen, the comedy of manners when adapted to the novel form tends to make only rather gross discriminations among manners and characters. Burney, for example, describes extremes of vulgarity, affectation and naïveté, and she exhibits these extremes in comic confrontations with each other and with polite behaviour. As a result, although she may distinguish between various forms of affectation (in *Cecilia*, among the sects of the 'supercilious', 'voluble', 'jargonists' and 'insensiblists', so classified by Mr Gosport at the Pantheon assembly [IV, vi; II, 192–3]), she does not similarly distinguish differences in polite behaviour. Instead, she takes polite behaviour for granted, or at least is not interested in particularizing it. In Burney's novels, good breeding is portrayed in chiaroscuro: it can shine by contrast only, and one result of this technique is that Burney's ballrooms and drawing-rooms are overstocked with vulgarians. Samuel Johnson highly approved this technique. The vulgarians who delighted him so much in *Evelina* are, in his view, successful only because they shine by contrast. Burney has recorded his pronouncement that the 'comic humour of character ... owes its effect to contrast; for without Lord Orville, and Mr Villars, and that melancholy and gentleman-like half-starved Scotchman, poor Macartney, the Brangtons, and the Duvals, would be less than nothing; for vulgarity, in its own unshadowed glare, is only disgusting'.[7] Johnson evidently does not regret that the comedy of manners in Burney's novels is always raucous, and never aims at or allows those fine discriminations between well-bred men and women that Richardson and Austen deal with.

Richardson's interest in drawing fine distinctions among characters is obsessive, but even in *Sir Charles Grandison* he does not rely on conventionally good manners to indicate moral stature. He is eager, first, to portray the manners of 'high life' accurately, in order to offer through his exemplary characters some prescriptions of his own for truly polite behaviour. He must therefore show himself and his characters to be familiar with the conventional code of manners, not violating it. But since he was not familiar with the more minute or stylized conventions of good society, he relied on his 'polite' correspondents to correct details of social usage in his novels.[8] A prescriptive attitude toward conduct or manners is characteristic of Richardson and his audience, and is thus very prominent in his novels. This prescriptiveness distinguishes Richardson's concern with accuracy in presenting the minutiae of manners from Austen's. She is as concerned that every detail she includes be correct. She revised inexact detail of this sort (for example, introducing a country surgeon to a lord) in her niece Anna's manuscript novel (*L*, p. 394). But she does not share Richardson's didacticism about manners: whatever didactic intentions she has, Austen makes no effort to prescribe the manners or conduct appropriate to every occasion of domestic life. When Richardson writes to a correspondent (who is actually urging him to extend *Grandison* beyond its seven volumes) that, 'By what we have seen of *both* [Sir Charles and Harriet], we know how they will behave on every future call or occasion,'[9] it is only too true.

Richardson does explore at least one serious and elaborate social form for his social comedy, the compliment, a form Austen's novels also exploit from time to time. Mr Collins's 'little elegant compliments as may be adapted to ordinary occasions' (68) typify her broadly comic attitude in the early novels, while the treatment of compliments in *Emma* is incalculably more complex. Differences in manners, and more, are registered, and assist in defining the characters who are exposed to them as well as those responsible for them. Furthermore, all the concern with flattery and compliments culminates, like so much in the novel, in Mr Knightley's proposal: 'I cannot make speeches, Emma' (430). The powerful emotional and thematic significance Austen can extract from so (apparently) insignificant a social form, while preserving a comic tone throughout, becomes even more astonishing when compared to Richardson's similar attempt in *Grandison*. His (and his characters') scrutiny of compliments and the motives behind them becomes so serious, so anxious, so full of meaning, so obsessive finally, that comedy is undermined. The obsessiveness insists only too much on the connection between manners and morals, so that comic confrontations and comic release are nearly impossible.

This obsession with compliments might be expected from an author who was notoriously greedy for praise and who died, according to Samuel Johnson, 'merely for want of change among his flatterers'.[11] In justice to Richardson's intense concern with ulterior motives for compliments, his early exposure to the disingenuousness which can underlie conventional formulae should be remembered. In his biographical letter to Johannes Stinstra he reveals that at thirteen he was party to ladies' 'Love Secrets' and was writing letters for them: 'I have been directed to chide, & even repulse, when an Offence was either taken or given, at the very time that the Heart of the Chider or Repulser was open before me, overflowing with Esteem & Affection; & the fair Repulser dreading to be taken at her Word' (*SL*, p. 231). Richardson's tone is light, but still registers the same consciousness of deception and awareness of the need for self-protection which accompany analyses of compliments in *Grandison*, qualifying the comic incongruities revealed. Thus Harriet, having arrived in London, recalls her friends' wishes that she will acquaint them with all the admiration she receives, and her uncle's comment that 'The vanity of the Sex . . . will not suffer any thing of this sort to escape our Harriet'. She is led from this lightness immediately to a serious reflection, the first of several on the subject:

It is true, my Lucy, that we young women are too apt to be pleased with the admiration *pretended* for us by the other Sex. But I have always endeavour'd to keep down any foolish pride of this sort, by such considerations as these: That flattery is the vice of men: That they seek to raise us in order to lower us, and in the end to exalt themselves on the ruins of the pride they either hope to find, or inspire: That humility, as it shines brightest in an high condition, best becomes a flatter'd woman of all women: That she who is puffed up by the praises of men, on the supposed advantages of person, answers *their end* upon her; and seems to own, that she thinks it a principal part of *hers*, to be admired by them: And what can give more importance to them, and less to herself, than this? (I, v; I, 18–19).

This analysis of men's motives in paying compliments, and the dangers women run in accepting them, is only preliminary. The form of a compliment, the manner of its delivery, and above all the manner of its reception, are felt to supply significant information about the characters responsible for them: about their manners, their perception, even at times their moral worth. This social form *can* serve, then, as a reliable index to character in Richardson's novels, and the main characters, who so often hear their own praises, are very much aware that this is so. They therefore feel a need for careful calculation and scrutiny of their responses to compliments. When Lady Betty, a new acquaintance in London, claims that she expects to be 'equally delighted and improved' by Harriet's company, Harriet is wary:

> I bowed in silence. I love not to make disqualifying speeches; by such we seem to intimate that we believe the complimenter to be in earnest, or perhaps that we think the compliment our due, and want to hear it either repeated or confirmed; and yet, possibly, we have not that pretty confusion, and those transient blushes, ready, which Mr Greville archly says are always to be at hand when we affect to disclaim the attributes given us.
>   Lady Betty was so good as to stop there; tho' the muscles of her agreeable face shewed a polite promptitude, had I, by disclaiming her compliments, provok'd them to perform their office (I, v; I, 22).

This interaction is complex. Even between women, the giving and receiving of compliments may be a snare for vanity and manipulation. When compliments occur between men and women, however, the stakes are higher, for compliments are prescribed in two antithetical social contexts: they belong to formal courtship ('paying addresses'), and they belong to gallantry and coquetry, what Richardson calls 'polite raillery', and what 'no English word but flirtation could very well describe', as Austen puts it in *Emma* (368). Serious 'intentions' or mere mockery may lie behind a compliment, but in either case, the conventional stance of the person who receives it is disbelief, a stance which may compromise one's sincerity and in any case asks for a repetition of the offence. Harriet's response when Sir Hargrave proposes to her sheds some interesting light on the resulting intricacy of these forms:

> I would have played a little female trifling upon him, and affected to take his professions only for polite raillery, which men call *making love* to young women, who perhaps are frequently but too willing to take in earnest what the wretches mean but in jest; but the fervour with which he *renewed* (as he called it) his declaration, admitted not of fooling; and yet his *volubility* might have made questionable the sincerity of his declarations. As therefore I could not think of encouraging his addresses, I thought it best to answer him with openness and unreserve (I, xvii; I, 83).

Pretended disbelief, or 'trifling', would be in order only if Harriet were planning to encourage Sir Hargrave. The exchanges of compliments that form the surface of polite conversation in Richardson's novels and which are, above all, required in the encounters of men and women, are an extremely complex social form, whose complexity derives from the conflicting motives it can accommodate. Sincerity, insincerity, perception, consideration, deviousness, vanity, hypocrisy, vulgarity, delicacy, manipulation – all these may be contained within and revealed below the smooth surface of the forms of polite admiration. Thus these forms seem to be ideal for 'serious' comedy, the comedy of manners which reveals character.

Richardson does extract from the forms some comedy of this sort, as when Sir Hargrave is introduced:

> for he forgets not to pay his respects to himself at every glass; yet does it with a seeming consciousness, as if he would hide a vanity too apparent to be concealed; breaking from it, if he finds himself observed, with an half-careless, yet seemingly dissatisfied air, pretending to have discover'd something amiss in himself. This seldom fails to bring him a compliment: Of which he shews himself very sensible, by affectedly disclaiming the merit of it; perhaps with this speech, bowing, with his

spread hand on his breast, waving his head to and fro – By my Soul, Madam (or Sir) you do me too much honour.

Such a man is Sir Hargrave Pollexfen. . . . He would have it that I was a perfect beauty, and he supposed me very young – Very silly of course: And gave himself such airs, as if he were sure of my admiration.

I viewed him steadily several times; and my eye once falling under his, as I was looking at him, I dare say, he at that moment pity'd the poor fond heart, which he supposed was in tumults about him; when, at the very time I was considering, whether, if I were obliged to have the one or the other, as a punishment for some great fault I had committed, my choice would fall on Mr Singleton, or on him (I, xi; I, 45–6).

Harriet's observations and attitudes must have delighted Austen. In *Emma*, the heroine's attitude toward Mr Elton similarly combines close observation with ironic reflection. When Mr Elton praises Emma's drawing, her 'inimitable figure-pieces', Emma's thoughts indicate her own amused detachment but her response feeds his vanity, as Harriet Byron's does Sir Hargrave's: 'Yes, good man! – thought Emma – but what has all that to do with taking likenesses? You know nothing of drawing. Don't pretend to be in raptures about mine. Keep your raptures for Harriet's face. "Well, if you give me such kind encouragement, Mr Elton, I believe I shall try what I can do" ' (43–4). Such examples show Austen's comedy to be more powerful than Richardson's even at his best, not simply because she dramatizes it more, the usual explanation. She learns in *Mansfield Park* and *Emma* to make each incident express more and more comic or emotional incongruity. Emma's delusions about Mr Elton's love for Harriet Smith, which spring from her own vanity, complicate this incident and create in the reader a combination of distance with engagement that Richardson's account of Harriet and Sir Hargrave does not demand.

The major difference between Richardson's and Austen's treatment of social forms, and particularly of 'polite raillery', is that, in this context at least, Richardson lacks a sense of play. He can allow Harriet's relations with Sir Hargrave to be amusing at first because Sir Hargrave is a fool, and Harriet is in no danger of being attracted to him. When he becomes the villain who has abducted Harriet, he can no longer be treated comically, and should not be; but Richardson's impulse to turn folly into villainy is characteristic. Sir Hargrave's future role in the action is predictable to anyone familiar with Richardson's work: having become the stock libertine, he pursues his unregenerate courses until he reaches a penitent deathbed. Richardson usually finds the relations between men and women either too threatening or else too easily assimilated to the conventions of melodrama for him to sustain a comic or playful tone. He is serious when he allows Sir Charles to say, 'Men and Women are Devils to one another. They need no other tempter' (II, xxxii; I, 439). *Grandison* begins as if Richardson can treat relations between the sexes comically, but Harriet's suitors soon become pathetic rather than comic, and her vanity, wit and social life decline as she falls in love, so that only characters who are almost uniformly good remain, and Richardson could not allow them to be coquettes. Austen is perfectly capable of exploring and rendering all the wilfulness or ugliness that can lie behind flirtation, as is evident in her treatment of the relations between Julia and Maria Bertram and Henry Crawford in *Mansfield Park*, or in her treatment of Frank Churchill and Emma at Box Hill. She is, however, equally capable of a number of other attitudes toward flirtation, ranging from her detached ridicule of its mindless vanity in Kitty and Lydia Bennet to her playful delight in Elizabeth's having 'dressed with more than usual care' for the ball at Netherfield and having 'prepared in the highest spirits for the conquest of all that remained unsubdued of [Wickham's] heart, trusting that it was not more than might be won in the course of the evening' (89).

Just as Richardson's attitude toward manners in his comedy generally lacks Austen's sense of play, his inclusion of revealing gestures in manner lacks her sense of structure. Although in *Grandison* he declares that in 'small instances ... are the characters of the heart displayed, far more than in greater' (III, xviii; II, 108), and in his letters that 'in the minutiae lie often the unfoldings of the Story, as well as of the heart' (*SL*, p. 289), his minutiae are essentially decorative, not structural: they create no real consequences for the plot. The 'small instance' he refers to is typical. Sir Charles, having rather abruptly left his circle in the drawing-room, takes the first opportunity to return, in order to explain that he is not really angry with anyone. The incident is edifying, not moving, and not important to the plot. It simply shows Sir Charles's moral virtue in yet another context. Austen, however, actually invents the 'illustrative' or characteristic gesture in manner which is also emotionally resonant or structural or both. Mr Knightley's asking Harriet to dance, to take the most famous example, is all three. It illustrates his character, including his complete superiority to Mr Elton. It relieves a painfully embarrassing situation, for Harriet, Mrs Weston, Emma and the reader; it also permits Emma to ask Mr Knightley to dance with her later, an incident highly charged with emotion because of Emma's unconscious love for him and

his conscious love for her, which he thinks unrequited. Finally, the incident has important consequences for the plot by allowing Harriet to think
herself in love with Mr Knightley, a development vital to the climax:
Emma's discovery of her love for Mr Knightley and their subsequent
engagement. Few gestures even in Austen's novels are so significant, but
those less embedded in plot can also have great power, as when in
Mansfield Park Edmund Bertram gives Fanny Price a gold chain, or Sir
Thomas orders her a fire although angry with her.

The sense of play and sense of structure which Austen brings to her
treatment of manners invests them with comic, emotional, moral and
thematic content that her predecessors cannot attain. Her finest
achievements in this mode occur in the later novels, although *Pride and
Prejudice* foreshadows some of the later mastery of small, significant
incident when Elizabeth unconventionally walks cross-country to visit
Jane, when Lady Catherine keeps Charlotte Collins outside by her
carriage, or when Darcy is silent and thoughtful at Longbourn near the
end. These incidents, although they point to Austen's later development,
do not fully anticipate it.

(ii) Wit and dialogue

The best effects in *Pride and Prejudice* are achieved because Austen
experiments with and masters other elements in the comedy of manners:
wit and dialogue. The two are distinct, though sometimes confused.
Dialogue may or may not be witty, while wit need not form part of
anything deserving the name of dialogue, which implies reciprocity: at
least in some sense, ideas and opinions are being exchanged among
reasonably attentive speakers, not merely displayed by them.

Whether wit appears in dialogue, so understood, or not, an author can
count on favourable responses to it and to characters responsible for it,
since pleasure in well-phrased judgments or criticisms, and in perceptions
or exposures of incongruity, is essentially an intellectual rather than a
moral response. If wit is to be registered as anything but delightful,
extremely skilful treatment is needed, like that in *Mansfield Park* and
Emma. Once Mr Knightley has rebuked Emma for the witty remark to
Miss Bates she 'could not resist' making (370), an engaged reader must
feel shock, embarrassment and even horror at Emma's wit. Austen's
treatment makes her remark then seem anything but witty. In *Pride and
Prejudice*, her demands on the reader's emotions in response to wit are less
complex and less strenuous, for her interest lies primarily in a more easily-
handled theme. She exposes the imperception rather than the ugliness

which pleasure in wit can produce. Nevertheless, she does demand that the reader register the inaccuracies of judgment encouraged by Elizabeth's wit. In her treatment of Mr Bennet, she requires a yet more complex response.

In Chapter II, Mr Bennet's wit displays his contempt for his wife and provokes her to expose herself before their children. Austen inserts this scene as a possible check to the reader's simple delight in Elizabeth's wit even before that delight can occur, for Elizabeth says nothing remarkable until Chapter IV. Although Chapter II is composed almost entirely of speeches, they do not constitute real dialogue. Mr and Mrs Bennet talk at cross-purposes. Mrs Bennet is wholly oblivious to her husband's mockery, but neither her idiocy nor her blindness can excuse him. Mr Bennet's wit seldom appears in dialogue whatever his company, for his ironic detachment usually precludes it. At the Netherfield ball, for example, he puts a stop to Mary's indifferent singing with an isolated remark, 'That will do extremely well, child. You have delighted us long enough. Let the other young ladies have time to exhibit' (101). When Elizabeth tries to persuade him to prevent Lydia's going to Brighton, he replies, 'Lydia will never be easy till she has exposed herself in some public place or other, and we can never expect her to do it with so little expense or inconvenience to her family as under the present circumstances' (230). This remark is as irresponsible as it is amusing. It is also firmly attached to the plot, for in Brighton Lydia does expose herself: she elopes with Wickham, an action that brings about the dénouement. The rest of the scene between Elizabeth and her father counterpoints her earnestness with his irresponsibility. Although in speaking to Elizabeth Mr Bennet can be serious, even affectionate, his detachment and withdrawal usually operate even then. His only 'dialogue' occurs at the end, when he appeals to Elizabeth to reconsider her engagement. Moved as he is in the scene, he quickly resumes his ironic stance once assured that Elizabeth loves Darcy.

Wit is, fortunately, more a part of dialogue in *Pride and Prejudice* than separable from it. Nothing could be more tedious, however, than dialogue (or narrative for that matter) composed entirely of epigrams, as some of George Meredith's novels too frequently testify. Although Austen herself refers to the 'epigrammatism of the general style' (*L*, p. 300), she has taken care that most of the wit be thematically significant and resonant beyond whatever immediate effect it creates. And the wit which she embeds in dialogue is at least as immediately delightful as Mr Bennet's and has far more complex uses in controlling the reader's response to the characters. The popular judgment that dialogue is the great achievement of *Pride and Prejudice* is certainly correct, although admiration is usually confined to its wit and its success in revealing character. Besides its entertaining and dramatic qualities, however, the witty dialogue among groups of characters in *Pride and Prejudice* gives fuller expression to feeling, perception and judgment, and consequently to the themes, than the dialogue of *Sense and Sensibility* and *Northanger Abbey* permits or intends. Without relinquishing earlier techniques of dialogue, Austen experiments with a number of new ones which allow increased expressiveness and which demand increasingly complex responses from readers. In *Mansfield Park*, *Emma* and *Persuasion*, the characters' talk is so much more carefully orchestrated and highly organized than in *Pride and Prejudice* that it should be distinguished by a more suggestive and wider term than dialogue: conversation. The conversations in the later novels are created by techniques fully evident in the dialogues of *Pride and Prejudice* but used with greater selectivity, density and economy, and thus with greater power.

One form of dialogue visible in *Pride and Prejudice* and *Sense and Sensibility* but eliminated later is a legacy from the eighteenth-century novel and supplies social comedy narrowly defined. A number of speakers expose their characteristic faults or foibles by their various responses to a particular event or topic. This form is very common in *Pride and Prejudice*. Chapter V, containing the five-way debate on pride, is a typical example. Some critics cite scenes like this one as evidence that Austen adopts a kind of relativism, but 'relativistic impressionism'[12] is hardly her aim. For her, and for the eighteenth century in general, human motives are fathomable, however complex; human judgments are corrigible, however prone to error; and human misconduct can be understood as folly and vice, not as their modern counterparts, neurosis and a secularized notion of original sin. Austen inherits a comic tradition which assumes that a complete, instructive and morally useful picture of society can be obtained by bringing together characters who exhibit manners, follies and affectations carefully chosen to contrast with each other as much as possible. The plays of Congreve and the novels of Fielding and Burney supply social comedy or the comedy of manners in this narrow sense. The form has undeniable virtues. It allows fools like Mrs Bennet to expose their folly with wonderful economy, while wits like Elizabeth shine by comparison. It can even be used if the follies of rational characters are to be displayed, as in *Sense and Sensibility* when Marianne's amusing notion that Colonel Brandon at thirty-five is too old and infirm to love is contrasted with the more accurate views of Mrs Dashwood and Elinor (37–8). But the broad, glaring contrasts essential to this form of dialogue disqualify it for the finer discriminations among feelings, perceptions and judgments which are Austen's major interest and which the new techniques of *Pride and Prejudice* accommodate.

These new techniques may be divided into two classes according to the effects they produce on the reader. First, effects may be immediate, and will depend on what the reader knows that the characters do not. Or effects may be delayed, and will depend on what the reader either can know but for various reasons does not realize (e.g., that Wickham's account of Darcy is fake), or what he simply cannot know until a later point in the novel or until a second reading. A good example of this last class is linear irony which does not stem directly from Elizabeth's misunderstanding of Darcy and Wickham: Elizabeth's shock at Charlotte's engagement set against Jane's later shock at Elizabeth's. The difference between this sort of linear irony and earlier structural ironies in Austen's work is interesting. The discussion of Colonel Brandon's 'infirmity' in *Sense and Sensibility* does create structural irony, for Marianne, having thought that Colonel Brandon, 'if he were ever animated enough to be in love, must have long outlived every sensation of the kind' (37), marries him at last, although he is a man 'whom, two years before, she had considered too old to be married, – and who still sought the constitutional safeguard of a flannel waistcoat' (378). In this instance, irony produces a comic effect independent of the novel's thematic concern with distinguishing sensitive, considerate behaviour from insensitivity and self-indulgence. In *Pride and Prejudice*, however, ironies of structure recur and are intimately connected with the theme, humbling pride of judgment.

Austen's ability to make dialogue serve her themes is not confined to the delayed effects supplied by linear irony or by such *tours de force* as Wickham's first conversations with Elizabeth. Most of the dialogue in *Pride and Prejudice* creates immediate effects, either those comic effects typical of eighteenth-century social comedy, or more complex ones which depend on what the reader knows that the characters do not. These complex effects are both emotional and comic. They increase in power the more the reader 'knows' – the more attention he pays – and are Austen's signature and her triumph. The reader has every incentive to read closely, for the more he is aware of the characters' motives, reactions, and misconceptions, the funnier the comedy. And the perfect lucidity with which unstated emotions and judgments display themselves to an attentive reader gives him that illusion of engagement with life which great art always produces by being clear, highly organized and complex where life is opaque and incoherent. *Pride and Prejudice* is a great work insofar as its brilliant lucidity transcends the complexity of life. But it is a puzzling and even flawed work if compared to Austen's later novels, insofar as its lucidity can also be excessive and glaring, violating life. When Austen writes mere social comedy, like that of Chapter V, character is necessarily simplified, for the effect depends on broad contrasts; characters merely personify different manners and attitudes. Such comedy is too lucid. When Austen writes her own higher comedy in *Pride and Prejudice*, she succeeds in permitting characters to expose, beneath the surface restraints of polite, clever talk, their unstated and incongruous (or clashing) motives, judgments and feelings. The range of comic and emotional incongruity which Austen learns to make her dialogue convey and her readers perceive in *Pride and Prejudice* is nicely illustrated, on the one hand, by the early scenes at Netherfield and, on the other, by Darcy's first proposal to Elizabeth.

The dialogues at Netherfield reveal incongruities in manners, motives and judgments which the reader registers as largely comic, although discrepancies and incongruities in feeling inevitably accompany them. This form of dialogue never permits merely comic incongruity; emotional incongruity always complicates the comedy.[13] Sometimes, indeed, emotional incongruity is the source of comedy: the discrepancy between Miss Bingley's interest in Darcy and his perfect indifference to her is wholly comic, as is Miss Bingley's jealousy of Elizabeth. The discrepancy between Darcy's interest in Elizabeth and her dislike is, however, more complex in its effects. When Darcy and Elizabeth identify each other's faults of character, the scene is principally comic, for each complacently misunderstands the other's meaning and motives, and the reader knows more than either can. Such comedy is central to the themes and plot of the novel, for Darcy's fault is 'a propensity to hate every body' and Elizabeth's 'wilfully to misunderstand them' (58). Yet the scene has undercurrents of sexual antagonism and attraction not entirely contained by the comedy of misjudgment enacted on the surface or by the linear irony which allows Elizabeth's and Darcy's judgments of each other to be felt again and again throughout the novel.

This form of dialogue, the source of what may be called Austen's high comedy, is perfectly illustrated by the scene which takes up the first half of Chapter X. The dialogue opens comically, develops emotional undertones and thematic implications through a variety of new techniques, and ends with a higher, more complex comedy than anything promised by its beginning. Austen prefaces this scene by noting that Darcy is writing to his sister, Miss Bingley is praising his efforts, and Elizabeth is 'sufficiently amused' by their 'curious dialogue, . . . exactly in unison with her opinion of each' (47). The reader should allow this observation to guide his understanding of the entire scene. He should notice that nothing Darcy says shakes Elizabeth's opinion of his pride, conceit and ill temper. The dialogue is so skilfully contrived, however, that while a prejudiced mind, like Elizabeth's, can see these qualities in Darcy's remarks, an open mind will not. When Darcy replies to Miss Bingley's inane question, 'do you always write such charming long letters', with 'They are generally long; but whether always charming, it is not for me to determine', a reader can take its politely repelling irony as evidence that Darcy, neither seeking nor liking Miss Bingley's flattery, puts up with it and her remarkably well.[14] The reader, of course, is better able than Elizabeth to interpret Darcy's behaviour correctly, having information she has not: that Darcy is attracted to Elizabeth and is as well-acquainted with Miss Bingley's jealousy as with her designs on him. These emotions have been amply demonstrated by Darcy's earlier pointed (but still polite) rebuke to Miss Bingley's catty remarks about Elizabeth: 'there is meanness in *all* the arts which ladies sometimes condescend to employ for captivation. Whatever bears affinity to cunning is despicable' (40). Yet ambiguity is not entirely dispelled by such speeches. A reader can take Darcy's remarks here and in Chapter X as Elizabeth would: evidence of ill-mannered conceit. His appreciation of the finer comedy in these scenes is simply delayed, and the immediate effect for him is purely comic. But it ought to be more complex. The reader should be able to see Darcy as politely, forbearingly ironic in his reception of Miss Bingley's officious compliments and should be aware that Elizabeth is viewing the same behaviour as evidence of his rudeness and his pride. Thus, the reader is asked to respond at several levels.

If the reader fails to be conscious of these incongruities, they are felt at last as linear ironies in the novel's comic attack on pride of judgment. The unconscious reader is but the more closely implicated. At the close of *Pride and Prejudice*, Elizabeth is able to reinterpret Darcy's behaviour, explicitly recognizing what she would not see earlier, although she could have seen it, as should the reader. She tells Darcy, 'You were disgusted with the women who were always speaking and looking, and thinking for *your* approbation alone' (380). Linear irony allows Austen to create comedy in which nothing is lost.

As the scene in Chapter X progresses, its demands on the reader increase. Miss Bingley's flattery peaks: 'a person who can write a long letter, with ease, cannot write ill' (48). Bingley is moved to interrupt with the first of several jokes he makes in this scene at Darcy's expense:

'That will not do for a compliment to Darcy ... because he does *not* write with ease. He studies too much for words of four syllables. – Do not you, Darcy?' A dramatization of Bingley's and Darcy's friendship follows. Their affectionate exchange could modify Elizabeth's earlier judgment that Darcy 'was only the man who made himself agreeable no where' (23), but does not. The reader must register her obliviousness while he takes in the two men's friendly, bantering discussion of Bingley's character, to which Elizabeth contributes twice. This discussion begins with a casual reference to essential differences between Bingley and Darcy. Darcy remarks that his style of writing is 'very different' from Bingley's. Miss Bingley cites her brother's careless and blotted letters, and he declares, 'My ideas flow so rapidly that I have not time to express them – by which means my letters sometimes convey no ideas at all to my correspondents' (48). Elizabeth takes the opportunity to praise Bingley for his humility, a quality she believes that Darcy conspicuously lacks. The reader should observe that all Elizabeth's speeches in this scene show her to be preoccupied with Darcy's character and with a desire to goad him. Darcy will not let her comment pass, observing that the 'appearance of humility ... is often only carelessness of opinion, and sometimes an indirect boast'. This Johnsonian distinction[15] amuses Bingley: 'And which of the two do you call *my* little recent piece of modesty?' Darcy's reply analyzes Bingley's character in a friendly, intimate, but also formal style: 'you are really proud of your defects in writing.... When you told Mrs Bennet this morning that if you ever resolved on quitting Netherfield you should be gone in five minutes, you meant it to be a sort of panegyric, of compliment to yourself – and yet what is there so very laudable in a precipitance which must leave very necessary business undone, and can be of no real advantage to yourself or any one else?' (49). Two new techniques of dialogue become apparent here. Austen allows her characters to refer to earlier conversations. And she allows the characters to debate as well as dramatize the central issue: judgment of character, in this case, Bingley's. The effects of these techniques are best understood, however, in relation to the entire scene, whose tensions increase enormously from this point.

Bingley's reply to Darcy's analysis is amused and friendly in tone, but after an initial laugh over remembering 'at night all the foolish things that were said in the morning', becomes rather self-justifying. He would, he says, leave Netherfield as quickly as he had claimed, and so 'did not assume the character of needless precipitance merely to shew off before the ladies' (49). Darcy, as a friend will, pursues his advantage. He is 'by no means convinced' that Bingley would leave so readily: 'if, as you were mounting your horse, a friend were to say, "Bingley, you had better stay

till next week," you would probably do it, you would probably not go –
and, at another word, might stay a month' (49). At this point, the witty
exchange between Darcy and Bingley has acquired a slight edge audible to
an attentive reader, but the tone remains good-humoured. Although
Darcy claims to know Bingley better than he does himself, in another
sense both men understand each other perfectly. The comedy of this
section arises from the discrepancy between their intimacy and Elizabeth's
obliviousness to it. She sees Bingley's sweetness without his amusement
at Darcy, and Darcy's arrogance without his affection for Bingley. She
believes herself to see more than either, as her next remark shows. She
tells Darcy, 'You have only proved by this ... that Mr Bingley did not
do justice to his own disposition. You have shewn him off now much
more than he did himself' (49). Once again, she is eager to praise Bingley
for a quality she thinks lacking in Darcy, but more important, she gives a
new and complex turn to the dialogue by addressing Darcy directly and
rather accusingly. From this point, Darcy's character is openly discussed
by Darcy and Elizabeth, although Bingley's character is still ostensibly
the principal subject. In this way, comic incongruity gives way to
emotional incongruity; the comedy of judgment openly and tacitly
enacted by the characters becomes more highly charged and more
complex; and the reader must register these judgments while adjusting
his own.

Bingley assists the shift in subject to Darcy's character. His reply to
Elizabeth begins genially and amusingly enough with, 'I am exceedingly
gratified ... by your converting what my friend says into a compliment
on the sweetness of my temper. But I am afraid you are giving it a turn
which that gentleman did by no means intend.' Sweet-tempered as he
certainly is, Bingley now displays some of the strain which always attends
being oneself a topic of conversation by inaccurately claiming that Darcy
'would certainly think the better of me, if under such a circumstance I
were to give a flat denial, and ride off as fast as I could'. Elizabeth's reply
perversely but wittily places the worst possible construction on this joke.
'Would Mr Darcy then consider the rashness of your original intention as
atoned for by your obstinacy in adhering to it?' Bingley refers her to
Darcy for an answer, and Darcy rightly observes that 'You expect me to
account for opinions which you chuse to call mine, but which I have
never acknowledged' (50). Whatever the reader's delight in Elizabeth's
wit, he ought to recognize her perverseness and her injustice, both of
which increase as her debate with Darcy continues; Darcy's increasing
(and pardonable) irritation is evident, of course, both to the reader and to
all the characters present.

Elizabeth at first refuses to argue the question Darcy raises. She wilfully

prefers to make pointed remarks about his character: 'To yield readily –
easily – to the *persuasion* of a friend is no merit with you.' Darcy ignores
her attack and her change of subject. He attempts to continue the
discussion as if it were rational and candid: 'To yield without conviction
is no compliment to the understanding of either.' Elizabeth's reply
constitutes her strongest criticism of Darcy in this scene and, in manner
typical of Austen's highest comedy, reflects upon her rather than him:
'You appear to me, Mr Darcy, to allow nothing for the influence of
friendship and affection.' Elizabeth herself has been allowing nothing for
the friendship and affection of Bingley and Darcy in her response to their
dialogue. Instead, every speech of both has been even more 'exactly in
unison with her opinion of each' than were the initial exchanges between
Miss Bingley and Darcy. At this point the reader must dissociate himself
from Elizabeth's prejudice. Her misreading of the dialogue is wilful, and
her attacks on Darcy are gratuitous. She is not the judge she thinks
herself. The reader does not feel these incongruities as comic ones,
however. The emotional undertones have become too serious, sharp and
powerful. Dialogue registers emotional incongruity rather than comic
incongruity whenever the more or less intense emotional undercurrents
which often lie beneath the surface of polite, witty talk are felt, to an
extent by the characters themselves, and to a greater degree by the reader.
The increasingly stilted dialogue testifies that Elizabeth and Darcy sense
these emotional tensions. Their argument has become a conflict of wills,
judgments and feelings; Bingley registers the reader's discomfort as well
as his own when he interrupts them.

The apparent subject of Elizabeth's and Darcy's dispute – openness to
persuasion in general and Bingley's in particular – is not a central issue in
the novel but does become important later in the action, when Bingley is
persuaded by Darcy that Jane does not love him and that he should leave
Netherfield. Linear irony controls every speech in this scene, but its
effects on this dispute are particularly complicated. Darcy will offer
Bingley more than 'one argument in favour of [the] propriety' (50) of
staying away from Netherfield and forgetting Jane, as his letter to
Elizabeth explains, but only the 'assurance . . . of your sister's
indifference' (hardly an argument) convinces Bingley that he should
remain in London (199). The humility in Bingley which Elizabeth praises
in Chapter X becomes his 'great natural modesty, with a stronger
dependence on [Darcy's] judgment than on his own', and allows him to
be too easily persuaded (199). Finally, Elizabeth claims very complacently
in Chapter X that she is 'not particularly speaking of such a case as you
have supposed about Mr Bingley. We may as well wait, perhaps, till

the circumstance occurs, before we discuss the discretion of his behaviour thereupon' (50). When the circumstance of Bingley's leaving
Netherfield does occur, however, it is no matter for rational argument.
Darcy's interference ruins Jane's happiness, and Elizabeth's angry
reference to it when Darcy proposes precludes any discussion of Bingley's
discretion.

Bingley's interruption of Elizabeth's exchange with Darcy brings the
discussion to a close, for the moment. His discomfort at their quarrel also
elicits from him an even more personal remark about Darcy than any of
those Elizabeth has been guilty of: 'I declare I do not know a more aweful
object than Darcy, on particular occasions, and in particular places; at his
own house especially, and of a Sunday evening when he has nothing to
do' (50-1). Elizabeth is considerate enough to check a laugh at this
reflection on Darcy because she 'thought she could perceive that he was
rather offended', despite his smile. The reader is well aware that Darcy's
offence is more likely to have proceeded from Elizabeth's remarks than
from Bingley's. The dialogue then closes quietly. Darcy acknowledges
Bingley's discomfort and his strategy by suggesting that Bingley wishes
to 'silence' the argument. Bingley agrees, still under the impression that
the argument is about him ('If you and Miss Bennet will defer [your
dispute] till I am out of the room, I shall be very thankful; and then you
may say whatever you like of me'). Elizabeth is quite ready to desist. And
Darcy resumes his letter, closing the scene with perfect symmetry.

Extended analysis makes this scene appear more solemn than it is.
Austen's touch is light and sure, allowing comic incongruity to modulate
brilliantly into a complex clash of wills, judgments and feelings, closing
in symmetry but not harmony, each character certain he understands
what has passed and confirmed in his original opinion of the others
despite all counter-evidence offered within this 'curious dialogue'. The
counter-evidence is twofold: Elizabeth, Bingley and Darcy reveal their
own characters while they discuss Bingley's, Darcy's and character in
general. Discussion of character becomes a common topic in *Pride and
Prejudice*, and frequently the character is present, as in this instance, to
bear a part in the debate. In Chapter X, all three debaters observe the
drama as well as participate in it, so that they are judging and responding
to each other's characters, just as the reader must. As a result, the reader
is asked to be aware of a threefold process of judgment when he reads the
dialogue. On the surface the characters are openly judging Bingley's
character. Tacitly, they are judging each other. And finally, the reader is
judging them. As one critic says of *Emma*, 'the process of reading runs
parallel to the life read about'.[16] This process is only intensified when

Darcy and Elizabeth discuss Darcy's character, pretending that Bingley's character is their subject. The reader must also register all the other elements in the dialogue: play of wit; talk on other important issues (character in general, persuasion, humility, pride); and comic and emotional incongruity acted out on qualities other than judgment (Miss Bingley's interest in Darcy, Darcy's and Bingley's friendship, Elizabeth's hostility to it). The technique of linear irony, variously implemented, requires further that the reader recall and re-estimate the scene at various points later in the novel. These requirements alone are quite sufficiently exacting. Added to them is the complex awareness of three processes of judgment, required by Austen's discovery that the characters can talk about judgment while enacting it.

The differences between a scene like this and one in which the topic of conversation is less charged, however thematic it may be, cannot be overemphasized. The debate on pride in Chapter V is apposite. In *Pride and Prejudice*, Austen can be seen in the process of discovering the technique of dialogue she exploits so successfully afterward, the technique of choosing topics for conversation which do not simply reveal differences among characters but which voice, dramatize and complicate the problems of judgment and sympathy which are the themes of the novels. This technique creates cumulative comic and emotional effects. Linear irony does permit these effects to be felt cumulatively in *Pride and Prejudice*, but in *Emma* and *Mansfield Park*, every speech and incident reflects back and forth upon every other. A web is created, not merely a line.

Another related and new technique is Austen's discovery that earlier discussions can be referred to and built upon in subsequent dialogues. This is a deceptively simple and obvious device, which only a great artist like Austen can use to advantage. It gives dialogue greater significance as well as verisimilitude. Characters do refer to previous conversations in the earlier novels, but their references serve different purposes. When Colonel Brandon exposes Willoughby's character to Elinor in *Sense and Sensibility*, he begins by asking her to recall an earlier conversation 'in which I alluded to a lady I had once known, as resembling, in some measure, your sister Marianne' (205). This lady was the near relation whom he had loved and lost, and whose illegitimate child had been seduced by Willoughby. But Colonel Brandon's early allusion to the lady is simply meant to prepare the reader for the later revelation. Austen prescribes just such preparation in advice to a niece who is writing a novel. 'St. Julian's History was quite a surprise to me; You had not very long known it yourself I suspect,' she observes; 'Had not you better give some hint of St. Julian's early history in the beginning of the story?' (*L*, p. 421). In *Pride and Prejudice*, however, references to earlier conversations help to create two significant new effects: a sense of interconnection between the dialogues which grants them a cumulative effect; and a sense that what is said by the characters is as important as what they do or experience.

A few critics have, like Norman Page, noted that *Pride and Prejudice* is 'to an appreciable extent, not so much about what is done as about what is said'.[17] Others have noted that the conversations bear a close relation to the structure and themes. But these critics tend to focus on the linear irony which the dialogues create, or on analysis of the characters' styles of speech. Certainly these repay analysis; but the most important technical discoveries for increasing the weight and the significance of dialogue in this novel are even more simple and direct. One of Austen's most significant discoveries is that without violating decorum, surprisingly direct statements, either about emotions or revealing them, can be made; that these statements produce a much higher emotional temperature than most comedy permits; but that these powerful emotions can still be contained within a comedy of misjudgment and error.

The dialogues in the three later novels (properly, conversations) form one of Austen's most powerful devices to engage and control her readers' responses, for she becomes increasingly skilful in rendering the conscious and unconscious complexities of feeling which the clever and civilized conversation of a roomful of people will partially convey and partially conceal. She seems to have attempted such a scene in *Sense and Sensibility*, when Elinor and Marianne dine at Mrs John Dashwood's London residence and meet Edward Ferrars' mother. Mrs Ferrars and Mrs John Dashwood slight Elinor and flatter Lucy Steele, ignorant of Lucy's engagement to Edward and fearing that Edward and Elinor are lovers. Though all the characters are completely at odds, full of misconceptions and of incompatible feelings and designs, the scene is not particularly moving or effective, for it is isolated. Emotional incongruity is best felt only as a cumulative effect. To orchestrate dialogues or conversations so that they are not isolated is a formidable achievement, and one which helps define the greatness of *Mansfield Park* and *Emma*. Austen acquires there the capacity to organize the feelings and judgments of more than two characters at once, whereas in *Pride and Prejudice* she does not really attempt to extend this exacting treatment of dialogue beyond the encounters of Elizabeth and Darcy, beginning at Netherfield and continuing to Darcy's second proposal.

Pride and Prejudice does approach *Emma* in density and power at the end, in the dialogues of Elizabeth and Darcy once they are engaged. Until then, their encounters are governed by some misconception about each other. An extreme of emotional incongruity is provided by Darcy's first proposal, for example, although the dialogue does register the cross-purposes in manners, motives and judgments which usually produce the principally comic incongruities of the drawing-room scenes at Netherfield and Rosings. The emotional content of this scene precludes comedy, however. The dialogue demands complicated, even contradictory responses in feeling and judgment from the reader. When Darcy first proposes, readers must rejoice in the criticisms he receives, for he richly deserves them, yet because his love for Elizabeth also endears him to the reader, her humiliating rejection is painful. Sympathy and judgment, pain and pleasure, are evoked together and reinforce each other, producing in the reader an intensity and complexity of feeling which approach Elizabeth's own at the end of the scene.

Once Elizabeth and Darcy are engaged, they are free to discuss, compare and reinterpret everything that has happened between them – particularly the origin and progress of their love. These last exchanges constitute the final stage of dialogue evident in the novel and create an entirely new effect. Ambiguity is dispelled, and release and intimacy effected, to a degree equalled only at the end of *Emma* and touched on at the end of *Persuasion*. This release is an achievement so peculiar to Austen's novels that calling it a 'stage' of dialogue is almost an indignity: it is rather a triumph of dialogue, something even Austen does not always accomplish, as *Persuasion* shows,[18] but which no earlier novelist begins to approach. The triumph lies in actually rendering through conversation a relationship which wholly convinces and satisfies the imagination, the mind and the heart, that a 'happy ending' (the most hackneyed of literary conventions, yet the least common in serious art) has been not merely asserted or conjured up, but actually achieved.

At the end of *Pride and Prejudice*, literary convention and social convention unite in a marriage which fulfils all the demands of imagination and of personality: mutual affection and intimacy. Intimacy or knowledge produces an acceptance which goes beyond judgment (and all former misjudgments) to affection. In the light of affection, even Darcy's unpreparedness to laugh at himself is an amiable blemish, sure to disappear in Elizabeth's company. In Austen's work, the comedy of manners (including the social and literary conventions which govern it, and the dialogue and conversations which shape it) increasingly allows the fullest expression and development of character, for her comedy is successful and expressive in direct proportion to her mastery of convention, especially dialogue. In *Pride and Prejudice*, the final conversations of Elizabeth and Darcy ratify their intended marriage. This marriage affirms a literary and social convention which gives to judgment and sympathy their most solid, stable, and indeed highest form – affection and intimacy – and confirms that in life and in literature conventions need not be limitations: they are a resource, not a restraint, for the human spirit.

3. THE ACHIEVEMENT OF *PRIDE AND PREJUDICE*

Pride and Prejudice climaxes a complicated first stage in Austen's astonishingly coherent and sustained artistic development. That development is based upon her highly sophisticated awareness of the reader's possible responses to fiction and upon her desire to exploit, through increasingly sophisticated techniques, the possibilities for manipulating, controlling and educating those responses, particularly sympathy and judgment. *Northanger Abbey* concerns itself with manipulating the less difficult but parallel responses to literature, distress and suspense. In *Sense and Sensibility*, sympathy and judgment are elicited, controlled and educated by the elaborate technique of contrast which informs the novel. *Pride and Prejudice* has even more complex designs upon its readers' sympathies and judgments. It assimilates the technique of contrast to a more highly-organized structural principle, linear irony, in order to subject pride of judgment to subversive treatment. The phrase 'pride of judgment' suggests the connections (explored by all Austen's succeeding novels) between the operations of critical and moral judgment and the operations of feelings like pride or delight in wit and charm. These connections are examined in the readers as much as in the characters. Wit and dialogue create a comedy of manners which encourages readers to form confident first impressions of character (without dictating them) and to assent to Elizabeth's judgments (without insisting on them). Subsequently, the structures which contain the comedy of manners – the techniques of contrast and of linear irony – undermine those impressions and judgments which the comedy has invited; the reader's judgment is as chastened at the end as Elizabeth's.

This subversive treatment of judgment is not cynical. Although the novel relentlessly exposes the fallibility of judgment, it also insists on educating and refining it. Its success in doing so signifies that Austen has triumphantly assimilated and transcended not merely her own prior achievements in the novel but those of her predecessors, Burney and Richardson. *Cecilia* and *Sir Charles Grandison* only partially succeed as comic novels incorporating the eighteenth-century didactic aim formulated by Samuel Johnson: to teach the passions to move at the command of virtue. *Pride and Prejudice* realizes this aim, as far as it can be realized in a novel. All three novels do, however, have certain literary devices in common, particularly the comedy of manners. *Cecilia* and *Grandison* also anticipate Austen's novels in using techniques of contrast to embody their themes and in showing traces of the technique of linear irony. *Grandison* shares the thematic device central to Austen's novel, an attempt to manipulate first impressions of character. But the comedy of manners in Richardson's and Burney's novels does not profit from these structural and thematic devices as Austen's does. The earlier novelists have a sense of structure but do not apply it systematically to their comedy. The sense of play and the economy of Austen's comedy are equally foreign to Richardson and to Burney.

These are serious and significant differences. Yet perhaps *Pride and Prejudice* is more successful than *Cecilia* and *Grandison* largely because Austen is more penetrating than either Burney or Richardson in her understanding of the relations among fiction, readers, passions and virtues. While she shares eighteenth-century views of the purpose of fiction, she does not accept any of the false assumptions or conventions these views entailed, notably that readers will helplessly imitate the actions of characters in novels. She is not persuaded that fiction can or should be exemplary. She recognizes instead that a novel is likely to produce effects in the mind only, and seldom there: mental habits are as tenacious as any, and stock responses can be confidently expected of readers in preference to any others. A novelist can combat these responses and, with difficulty, educate them, but only if they are wholly understood, anticipated and allowed for, as they are in all of Austen's novels. In *Pride and Prejudice*, Austen intentionally uses eighteenth-century literary devices to an eighteenth-century end, moral and emotional didacticism.

The greatness of *Pride and Prejudice* remains undefined. If it were Austen's last novel, it would be considered a perfect work of its kind, not to be surpassed. No possibility of transcending its achievements could be imagined if *Mansfield Park, Emma* and *Persuasion* had not followed it. Nevertheless, *Pride and Prejudice* does anticipate the characteristic triumph of these greater novels, an ability to create intimacy with and absorption in their characters and their worlds. The last three novels extend and improve upon the techniques of *Pride and Prejudice*, whose theme and the methods embodying it dictate unremitting exposure to the characters and especially to their talk, which provides the fullest possible understanding of them. Yet any attempt to determine whether the theme suggested the possible shape and uses of the structure and the dialogue or whether, on the other hand, the form preceded the matter, is more than usually futile, so well do they mesh and so perfect is the effect: absolute absorption in the world created.

Conclusion
The Later Novels

The best of Austen's immediate predecessors and contemporaries in the novel create domestic and moralizing fiction which is highly patterned and explicitly didactic, although with substantial elements of more subtle literary art. Austen's triumph in her early novels is to assimilate their achievements and to better them so that her own fiction realizes their aims: to delight and instruct. Her ability to delight is undeniable; her didactic intentions less acknowledged. In the early novels, Austen discovers themes and techniques which engage and increasingly complicate the reader's judgments and sympathies. His emotions, perceptions and moral sense are exercised in an increasingly complete and realized world; his responses are jolted, tested and refined. Whether or not Q. D. Leavis is right to define the 'peculiar property of a good novel' as 'the series of shocks it gives to the reader's preconceptions', she is wrong to claim that George Eliot 'seems to have been the first novelist to be conscious of this most important function of the novel'.[1] Not only Austen but Sterne and Richardson anticipate Eliot in being fully aware of this possible effect of the novel and fully determined to exploit it. A more significant comparison between Austen and Eliot links them also to Henry James. They share a conviction that literary experience can and should result in an enlarged or enriched consciousness. However differently all three might define an 'enriched consciousness' and however diverse their means of achieving it, they all make problems of intellectual, moral and emotional responsiveness central issues in their novels. They all create characters difficult for readers to judge or to like, and then require complex combinations of judgment and sympathy, which readers can produce only by refining and educating their responses and consciousness.

This effect is especially characteristic of Austen's two later novels, which exhibit the same relation to her early novels as these in their turn show to earlier fiction. While technique seems to become invisible in *Mansfield Park* and *Emma*, demands and power intensify. The difficulty lies in isolating the techniques which account for the intensity and depth sensed by every reader of these novels, but they can in fact be located in

121

management of dialogue or conversation. In these novels, the responses of the characters to each other are orchestrated in conversations which combine incongruity and complexity of feeling with the greatest possible clarity. Accordingly, an attentive reader will find that these conversations make immense demands upon his emotional, moral and perceptual responses. Yet these complicated effects can be attributed on the whole to two very simple techniques which, taken together, improve enormously on the techniques of *Pride and Prejudice*: Austen carefully limits the number of subjects which appear in conversation, and she allows these subjects to be repeated frequently. For example, the same characters (or different ones) will take up and refer to subjects which have been discussed earlier. The second of these techniques is prominent enough in *Pride and Prejudice*; the first, however, is not.

Substantiating these claims requires something perilously close to the unlovely activity of word-counting. Nevertheless, if the subjects of conversation which occur in comparable pages from early chapters in each of the six novels are compared, the results are surprisingly revealing. They document the development in the techniques of conversation.

In *Northanger Abbey* (Chs. II–VIII; pp. 18–59), very little sustained conversation occurs. Sixteen separate subjects may be found in these pages, and only two repeat or extend earlier discussions; predictably, these two subjects are Bath society and novels. Other subjects range from journal keeping and female friendship to muslin gowns and the speed of horses. Conversation in *Sense and Sensibility* (Chs. IV–XI; pp. 19–57) is more sustained and homogeneous: two of the ten subjects recur (Edward Ferrars' feelings for Elinor and hers for him; Colonel Brandon's character) and all have some relation to each other and to the themes or plot (discussion of Edward's character, Willoughby's character, second attachments, 'catching men', love and marriage after age twenty-seven). In *Pride and Prejudice*, however, dialogue expands almost explosively: Chapters VI–XI (pp. 21–58) cover twenty-eight separable topics of conversation, only seven of which can be said to involve repetition. Most of these subjects are related to each other and to the themes, although many serve principally to allow characters to display themselves in Burneyan social comedy (the subjects of reading, libraries, accomplished women, town and country). Some of the repeated subjects directly serve the themes (faults of character, Bingley's openness to persuasion, manners), but others bear only indirect relations to the plot or the themes (dancing, Elizabeth's walk to Netherfield, her fine eyes). Although the homogeneity of *Sense and Sensibility* is absent, Austen's art here is nonetheless greater, for what the characters say on these several subjects forces the reader to register various degrees of comic and emotional incongruity, at least in those scenes which gather together some of the 'intricate characters' (*PP*, p. 42).

In Chapters III–VI of *Mansfield Park* (pp. 23–62), Austen's concern to make conversations serve the themes, reveal characters and produce cumulative effects is clear. Only fourteen subjects of conversation can be isolated. Four among them are repeated; most subjects are discussed by three or more characters; later conversations revert to almost all the subjects covered in these chapters; and later events reflect on every single one of them. For example, Fanny Price's projected move to the White house to live with Mrs Norris, a repeated subject, is successively discussed by Lady Bertram and Fanny, by Fanny and Edmund, and by Mrs Norris and Lady Bertram; Fanny's position at Mansfield is a central theme. The subject of improvements and planting, another repeated topic, is widely canvassed at dinner in Chapter VI. Although other topics intervene, Mrs Norris, Mr Rushworth, and Maria Bertram, Lady Bertram and Dr Grant, and Mary, Edmund, and Fanny take up the subject in succession, and it gains importance as the novel progresses. The justly-celebrated scenes at Sotherton stem from and enormously extend the implications of this earlier conversation.

Emma, however, brings all these techniques to a climax, as one might expect. In Chapters III–VII (pp. 20–56), only ten subjects of conversation occur, five of which echo earlier subjects. Furthermore, because these five themselves include repetition, the actual tally is even more impressive. Robert Martin's character, station and manners are discussed three times, Emma's influence on Harriet Smith twice, and Emma's 'likeness' of Harriet three times, leaving only two other topics: Mr Elton and his manners; and Emma, her character, looks and possible marriage. This list makes clear the almost single-minded concern with assessment of character in dialogue, and makes *Persuasion* seem even more anomalous than usual.

In Chapters III–VI (pp. 17–52) of *Persuasion*, conversation is so scarce that only five subjects appear, and no discussion explores character. If the next forty pages or so are examined instead, a more respectable result is obtained: in Chapters VII–X (pp. 53–92), ten subjects may be counted and, with some effort, two may be considered repetitions of the discussion of marriage in Chapter VIII (the subsequent conversations on the Crofts' marriage, and on the possible marriage of Captain Wentworth to one of the Musgrove girls). These conversations seldom include more than two or three characters, and although Anne hears all of them, she hardly ever contributes anything to discussion. The departure from *Emma* and from *Mansfield Park* could scarcely be more radical. Similarly, *Persuasion* makes fuller use than either of these novels of soliloquies, apostrophes, and reported, perfunctory conversations, in which a character's speech is quoted but no exchange of words occurs. Examples in Chapters III–VI are Anne's reflections on the Crofts' tenancy of Kellynch ('*he*, perhaps, may be walking here' [25]), her family's comments on her uselessness, the Musgroves' brief enquiries about Bath, Mary's complaints of illness and complaints about servants, comments on Anne's music, on the removal of the Crofts to Kellynch, and on the Crofts' connections. The similarly-placed segments in the other novels contain very few of these failed or avoided conversations. *Emma* has only one (Mr Woodhouse's polite offers of food to his guests); *Mansfield Park* three (Sir Thomas's exhortation to Tom, Mrs Norris's wonderful indignation at Mrs Grant's lavish housekeeping, and Sir Thomas's parting adjuration to Fanny); and *Pride and Prejudice* none. *Sense and Sensibility* and *Northanger Abbey* have a few, but not as many as *Persuasion*.

These observations reinforce impressions of the novels that most readers are likely to have formed already, such as a sense of Anne Elliot's isolation and repression, or of the thinner texture of *Persuasion* in comparison to *Mansfield Park* and *Emma*. Although this list of subjects is far from exact or objective – the topics of conversation in the later novels are especially fluid and hard to define – nevertheless, it does document Austen's mastery of the powerful device of repetition. In the later novels, every recurrence of a subject, perception or incident reflects back on and adds to the previous ones, producing a cumulative effect. In *Emma* particularly, subjects are treated with an almost musical sense of structure, recurring with much the same increase in tension and power as they do in a Bach fugue.

These observations also hint at other differences in techniques of dialogue, among them the higher and more direct emotional content of conversation in *Mansfield Park* and *Emma*. The differences may be examined by comparing the demands and effects on an attentive reader of a very brief passage from each of the later novels. The passages bear on a subject central to all the novels – judgment of character – and they are taken from the sections already examined, for if every effect in the last three novels is cumulative, earlier scenes are necessarily much simpler than later ones.

In Chapter III of *Mansfield Park*, fifteen-year-old Fanny Price is threatened with removal from Mansfield to live with her aunt, Mrs Norris. In a brief scene, she tells her cousin Edmund Bertram of 'her distress', and he attempts to reconcile her to the move, as she knows he will. Their exchange typifies the quality of this scene well enough, although selection inevitably does violence to the integrity of the whole. Edmund has just told Fanny that she will be important to her aunt, and as a result Fanny's character becomes the subject between them:

> 'I can never be important to any one.'
>
> 'What is to prevent you?'
>
> 'Every thing – my situation – my foolishness and awkwardness.'
>
> 'As to your foolishness and awkwardness, my dear Fanny, believe me, you never have a shadow of either, but in using the words so improperly. There is no reason in the world why you should not be important where you are known. You have good sense, and a sweet temper, and I am sure you have a grateful heart, that could never receive kindness without wishing to return it. I do not know any better qualifications for a friend and companion.'
>
> 'You are too kind,' said Fanny, colouring at such praise; 'how shall I ever thank you as I ought, for thinking so well of me? Oh! cousin, if I am to go away, I shall remember your goodness, to the last moment of my life.'
>
> 'Why, indeed, Fanny, I should hope to be remembered at such a distance as the White house. You speak as if you were going two hundred miles off, instead of only across the park' (26).

Even so brief a passage makes great demands on a reader's perceptions and feeling, that is, his judgment and sympathy. Of the two, the demands made upon judgment are rather less stringent. Edmund is evaluating Fanny's character, her strengths and limits, as part of another question requiring judgment: will it be to Fanny's advantage to live with Mrs Norris? The reader is asked, therefore, to judge how far Edmund's estimation first of her character and second of the advantages for her of living under Mrs Norris's care may be correct. Judgment is at issue between Fanny and Edmund and between them and the reader as well. And, as so often in *Mansfield Park*, judgment is confounded. The second of these issues remains undecided and unresolved in conversation (Fanny is not really convinced by Edmund), although not in action, for of course 'Mrs Norris had not the smallest intention of taking her' (28).

Linear irony is not at work here, for even on a first reading the reader is likely to anticipate this outcome. Mrs Norris's determination to do nothing for Fanny has been firmly established, and Edmund's willingness to credit the reverse despite his professed knowledge of her character ('I am glad her love of money does not interfere' [26]), seems intended to cast doubt on his judgment. Another technique used in *Pride and Prejudice*, parallels and contrasts among characters and incidents, is more visible: this scene is meant to be weighed against the other scenes in which Fanny's removal is discussed if the reader is to estimate Fanny's character and her position accurately. Lady Bertram's indifference to Fanny's leaving – except in the matter of tacking on her patterns (25) – gives weight to Fanny's bleak statement that she 'can never be important to any one', even though in a few years Fanny will be important enough to her aunt that Lady Bertram is 'sure I shall miss her very much' when she goes to Portsmouth (371). While motivated by selfishness, Mrs Norris's response to the White house plan ('Fanny live with me! the last thing in the world for me to think of, or for any body to wish that really knows us both' [28]), does seem a truer judgment on the desirability of the scheme than does Edmund's. More important, however, are the parallels to this scene which reverberate throughout the novel. Fanny's 'importance' or position at Mansfield is a central theme, dwelt on in the two preceding chapters and prominent afterward, reaching a kind of climax of horror when Mrs Norris rebukes her for refusing to act ('I shall think her a very obstinate, ungrateful girl, if she does not do what her aunt and cousins wish her – very ungrateful indeed, considering who and what she is' [147]), and a climax of squalor when Fanny is exiled to Portsmouth. If Fanny's character is to be understood by the reader, and if he is to feel for her properly, he must correctly judge her painful position at Mansfield and be conscious of all the difficulties she must contend with there. The early chapters give details of her youth in order to force the reader to estimate her position; the childhood of no other Austen heroine receives such attention.

The emotional demands made by this scene are much greater than those it makes upon judgment. Terms like emotional incongruity or comic incongruity, which work well enough to describe the effects of dialogue in *Pride and Prejudice*, seem inadequate here, partly because feelings are expressed so openly. Fanny's fears, sense of inferiority and gratitude, are expressed with almost overwhelming directness. Edmund's support and reassurance are equally direct. The reader is made to feel Fanny's distress, twice mentioned earlier in the scene, in all its strength; for her distress clearly has released her feelings of insecurity, vulnerability, anxiety and self-consciousness. The bleakness of 'I can never be important to any one' has all the poignancy of adolescent despair, which is to say, a touch of the self-indulgent and the exaggerated as well. More shocking is a similar statement she makes later in the same scene: 'If I could suppose my aunt really to care for me, it would be delightful to feel myself of consequence to any body! – *Here*, I know I am of none, and yet I love the place so well' (27). Edmund does not reassure her when he cannot. He does not reply to her that she is of consequence at Mansfield, which would be a lie; he only says that she will not lose everything. She will have the park, gardens and library to use as before, and the same horse to ride and people to see. Edmund's reassurance is of the best kind, honest as well as affectionate; readers who dislike his 'priggish' manner should pay more attention to his good nature and good feeling in relation to Fanny.

The reader of this brief exchange is asked to register Fanny's strong sense of being unloved, unwanted, foolish and awkward, coupled with her strong capacity for love: earlier in the scene she says, 'I love this house and every thing in it' (26), and Edmund speaks of her 'constant little heart' (27). The scene should make the reader feel Fanny's limits and strengths, both derived from the same source: her extreme capacity for feeling. Yet at the same time, the reader is asked to remain at some distance from her. Fanny's feelings have some of the excesses of self-conscious adolescence. When they overflow in this exchange ('Oh! cousin, if I am to go away, I shall remember your goodness, to the last moment of my life'), Edmund's reply combines affection with distance. Austen is asking that the reader fully register the strength of Fanny's emotions, while preserving a sense of their excess: in short, a poignant approach to comedy. She requires her readers to feel the same affectionate distance from Fanny that Edmund shows, but affection must predominate.

The response demanded for Fanny here and elsewhere in *Mansfield Park* does go against the grain of most readers' feelings, as Austen is aware. The weakly, retiring Miss de Bourgh in *Pride and Prejudice* testifies that Austen is perfectly conscious of how unattractive these qualities can be. To give them to a heroine along with such other equally unattractive qualities as adolescent self-consciousness, anxiety and fearfulness is a risk Austen deliberately runs. She intends to write a novel in which responses and judgment are highly problematic, for the characters and for the reader. Austen succeeds in evoking such complex, contradictory and fluctuating responses for each character that the book confuses most readers, largely because they do not think that the contradictions and the resulting anxieties are controlled or intended. Since Fanny Price is the heroine, and since she is 'well principled and religious' (294), therefore good, these readers assume that their own lack of unqualified sympathy for her indicates a failure in Austen's intention or execution.

On the contrary: Fanny Price is not meant to be a complete or model woman. She is subject to many of the errors common to adolescents. Within the novel, these errors are occasionally amusing or distancing, and are meant to be so. Fanny's lack of wit, charm and vitality is a thematic necessity. Only if she and Edmund are largely without these qualities can the Crawfords' charm be felt sufficiently to qualify their faults, so that they become equally difficult for Edmund and Fanny, and for the reader, to judge. Austen is deliberately separating goodness and charm. The novel depends upon a struggle between these two orders of attraction. The charming characters, Henry and Mary Crawford, find themselves attracted against their expectation and even against their will to the good characters. Edmund is attracted to Mary against his better judgment. And even Fanny, whose love for Edmund renders the attentions of Henry and Mary painful to her, finds herself feeling more for both than she expects or desires. The reader in turn feels for the judges all four, but uneasily, for Austen makes feeling and judgment even more difficult for the reader than for the characters themselves. She insists at almost every point on registering the characters' conflicting feelings and their opposing judgments of themselves and of each other; and she demands that the reader judge among them. An overriding concern with judgment in relation to feeling is the signature of *Mansfield Park* and accounts for both its tensions and its power. The presence of a character good, witty and utterly charming, like Elizabeth Bennet, would destroy the novel by dissipating its tensions, for in *Mansfield Park* a very delicate balance among the claims of the characters is required and sustained.

One of the best examples of this balance is visible in the treatment of Henry Crawford's courtship of Fanny. The reader experiences extraordinary difficulty in responding to Henry and to Fanny both; they invite sympathy and censure alternately. Fanny's feeling that 'She might have disdained him in all the dignity of angry virtue, in the grounds of Sotherton, or the theatre at Mansfield Park' (328) is shared by the reader to some extent, perhaps even exceeded, for the reader knows as Fanny cannot with what vain, selfish, 'idle designs' (292) Henry began to pay attention to her: 'I cannot be satisfied without Fanny Price, without making a small hole in Fanny Price's heart' (229). Yet what becomes his sincere love creates sympathy for him, in the reader as in Fanny:

He was now the Mr Crawford who was addressing herself with ardent, disinterested, love; whose feelings were apparently become all that was honourable and upright, whose views of happiness were all fixed on a marriage of attachment; who was pouring out his sense of her merits, describing and describing again his affection, proving, as far as words could prove it, and in the language, tone, and spirit of a man of talent too, that he sought her for her gentleness, and her goodness; and to complete the whole, he was now the Mr Crawford who had procured William's promotion! (328).

As a result, Fanny and the reader 'must be compassionate' (328), the reader rather more so, for Fanny's coldness and rejection create more sympathy for Crawford, and even some slight criticism of her – although one or two phrases in this remarkable passage can also put the reader on guard against Crawford. The manner in which Austen arranges that the reader will feel critical of Fanny while sympathizing with her typifies the methods of *Mansfield Park* in general. Austen has first made clear that the mode of Fanny's rejection was

so pitying and agitated, and words intermingled with her refusal [were] so expressive of obligation and concern, that to a temper of vanity and hope like Crawford's, the truth, or at least the strength of her in-difference, might well be questionable; and he was not so irrational as Fanny considered him, in the professions of persevering, assiduous, and not desponding attachment which closed the interview (328).

Having thus partially excused Crawford to the reader, she allows Fanny to be harsh:

Now she was angry. Some resentment did arise at a perseverance so selfish and ungenerous. Here was again a want of delicacy and regard for others which had formerly so struck and disgusted her. Here was again a something of the same Mr Crawford whom she had so re-probated before. How evidently was there a gross want of feeling and humanity where his own pleasure was concerned (328–9).

Thanks to Austen's preparations, the reader is unlikely to assent to this strong censure, however he may feel for Fanny's unfortunate position, being in love with one man and sought by another, and however correct he might otherwise think Fanny's judgment that to persist in an unwelcome courtship is ungenerous. But before the reader has time to adjust and weigh all his complex responses to so much highly-charged material (love, rejection, hope, anger, distress, indignation), all is undercut by: 'So thought Fanny in good truth and sober sadness, as she sat musing over that too great indulgence and luxury of a fire upstairs' (329).

Austen allows no easy responses, either of sympathy or judgment, to the characters or to the incidents in *Mansfield Park*. As Henry Crawford's courtship progresses, the reader's difficulties increase. At Portsmouth, he seems especially feeling and considerate. Fanny actually finds herself thinking of him seriously, as a result. She reflects that if she were able to return his affection, she would have been able, once married, to invite Susan to stay with her, for 'She thought he was really good-tempered, and could fancy his entering into a plan of that sort, most pleasantly' (419). Yet Austen allows her to reflect also, 'so very feeling as he now expressed himself, and really seemed, might it not be fairly supposed, that he would not much longer persevere in a suit to distressing to her?' (414). And Austen carefully points out that her perception of his improvement does not consider 'in how different a circle she had been just seeing him, nor how much might be owing to contrast' (413). This complex treatment allows Henry Crawford's elopement with Maria to seem credible, even though the reader's sympathies have been so recently excited for him. Equally credible is Austen's statement that 'Would he have persevered, and uprightly, Fanny must have been his reward – and a reward very voluntarily bestowed – within a reasonable period from Edmund's marrying Mary' (467).

The didactic intention of *Mansfield Park* depends very greatly on this complicated treatment of the characters and on these complex and difficult demands upon the reader's judgments and sympathies – which have been far from exhaustively described. *Mansfield Park* explores feeling in relation to conduct, judgment and principle in order to educate the reader into a fuller awareness of all three. The novel does not simply affirm the value of any one of these – not even principle. Austen investigates the costs, for social conduct and for moral judgment, of either underestimating the power of emotional life, or being excessively vulnerable to it, as Fanny is; and these costs are exacted from principled and unprincipled characters alike. The costs to Fanny are clear. The costs of neglecting or ignoring passion may be less obvious. Sir Thomas Bertram, for instance, Edmund, and Henry Crawford all underestimate and fail to allow for the nature and strength of Maria Bertram's feelings, as she herself does, and all suffer for the result in proportion as their conduct deserves. Edmund, who is 'not at all afraid for' Maria, despite Fanny's hints, 'after such a proof as she has given [by engaging herself to Mr Rushworth], that her feelings are not strong' (116), cannot see Maria's love for Crawford and does not prevent its consequences, either at Mansfield or at London. Her father sanctions her marriage despite perceiving her indifference to Mr Rushworth:

> Sir Thomas was satisfied; too glad to be satisfied perhaps to urge the matter quite so far as his judgment might have dictated to others. It was an alliance which he could not have relinquished without pain ... and if Maria could now speak so securely of her happiness with [Mr Rushworth], speaking certainly without the prejudice, the blindness of love, she ought to be believed. Her feelings probably were not acute; he had never supposed them to be so (201).

Henry Crawford, however, unprincipled and more selfish than either Edmund or Sir Thomas, loses the most by having 'put himself in the power of feelings on her side, more strong than he had supposed' (468).

The misjudgment and misconduct of Sir Thomas, one of the novel's most principled characters, should convince readers that Austen's subject is rather the perhaps unavoidable difficulties and limits of principle than its efficacy. Fanny, whose conduct and principle are consistently right, finds nonetheless that her feelings always complicate and perplex her judgments. When she thinks of her resolve not to act in *Lovers' Vows*, 'her doubts were increasing':

> Was she *right* in refusing what was so warmly asked, so strongly wished for? what might be so essential to a scheme on which some of those to whom she owed the greatest complaisance, had set their hearts? Was it not ill-nature – selfishness – and a fear of exposing herself? And would Edmund's judgment, would his persuasion of Sir Thomas's disapprobation of the whole, be enough to justify her in a determined denial in spite of all the rest? It would be so horrible to her to act, that she was inclined to suspect the truth and purity of her own scruples (153).

Fanny experiences some form of distress on almost every page of *Mansfield Park*; this instance is merely one of the more elaborate. Perhaps part of Austen's intention is to create a heroine whose complicated 'distress' is legitimate and genuine, not spurious as it is in the sentimental novel. Certainly Austen succeeds in making Fanny's position increasingly difficult as the novel progresses: she is more and more distressed. In the exchange quoted between Fanny and Edmund, on the other hand, although Fanny's distress is emphasized, the scene actually dramatizes something else. In it, Fanny and Edmund are entirely open and loving. Their affection is directly expressed and satisfies Fanny. Later, however, she loses Edmund insofar as his love is extended to Mary Crawford. Fanny is then in the false and painful position of receiving Edmund's brotherly confidences about his love for Mary when her own love for him is not that of a sister. Aware of her love and jealousy, Fanny can no longer be open with Edmund about her feelings and her judgments, particularly concerning Mary. She suffers from loss and from concealment, and only at the end is she relieved of both. This early, open exchange between Fanny and Edmund is necessary if the reader is to register fully the pain of her later loss and repression. Irony operates here in relation to feeling, not to judgment as in *Pride and Prejudice*, and the effect upon the reader is cumulative. In *Pride and Prejudice*, linear irony guarantees that the action will reverse or undercut almost every judgment, so that effects are felt cumulatively. But these effects are obtained through a linear or symmetrical structure, rather than by increasing the force of each successive misjudgment. Elizabeth's later judgments and reassessments systematically balance or cancel earlier ones. In *Mansfield Park*, on the other hand, each intimate conversation between Edmund and Fanny gains in emotional complexity and power as the discrepancy between the kind of love they feel for each other increases. Each later sign of Edmund's love, such as his gift of a gold chain, is both welcome and increasingly painful to Fanny, and each must be felt in relation to this early scene in which his love relieves her distress instead of augmenting it.

The dialogue and the narrative in *Mansfield Park* register powerful feelings on almost every page, usually painful ones like anxiety, uncertainty, jealousy and distress. These are felt cumulatively, far more strongly than any accompanying value the novel may suggest for peace and tranquillity. This powerful representation of feeling informs and complicates the novel's presentation of judgment also. Judgment occurs and is required on every page. As a result, the reader (like Fanny) can never relax. He must continually weigh and judge among the characters' different estimations of themselves and each other while his sympathies are being strongly solicited by them. He is, for example, attracted to the Crawfords' liveliness and wit; he is repelled by their coarseness and selfishness; he recognizes that they have never before met people as full of 'heart' as some of those at Mansfield, and that they are powerfully affected as a result (as Mary says, 'You have all so much more *heart* among you, than one finds in the world at large' [359]); and he feels for the various jealousies, anxieties and uncertainties that all the characters labour under, sometimes amused and sometimes appalled at the distance between their real and their professed feelings, motives and judgments. The tone of *Mansfield Park* is painfully anxious, in keeping with its didactic intention: to make the reader feel more than he ever has the complexity and difficulty of moral and emotional response to character.

The tone of *Emma* is otherwise, genial and expansive, in keeping with its different didactic intention. If *Pride and Prejudice* treats judgment comically and *Mansfield Park* treats it seriously, even obsessively, then *Emma* may be said to treat it almost in a cavalier manner. Austen asks the reader of *Emma* to exercise his judgment even more carefully and more strenuously in some ways than in *Mansfield Park*, and then requires him to transcend it altogether, in the interests of something greater: love. *Emma* creates a comedy of intimacy or of love which embraces all the characters, however irritating and exasperating they may be and however much they invite harsh judgment at first. Austen obliquely voiced this intention when she said, 'I am going to take a heroine whom no one but myself will much like,'[2] for of course she insists on each reader's liking Emma, however annoyed or critical he may also feel. Austen insists on similar complexity in the reader's responses to the other characters, notably Mr Woodhouse and Miss Bates, and most notably of all, Mrs Elton.

No character in all Austen's works is more exasperating, more impossible than Mrs Elton, who parodies all Emma's faults and has none of her virtues. She thinks herself the centre and leader of Highbury as Emma has done, but receives no parallel humiliation, for Austen allows her at the end to think as well of herself as ever, perhaps better. None of the other characters challenges her self-complacency: their good breeding forbids it, and they must therefore receive her impertinences with civility. Her speeches grate on the reader's nerves as much as on the characters'. Yet she has the last speech in the novel (although not the last word), indeed the only speech in the last chapter. Austen seems to be insisting on her presence even while she is asserting the 'perfect happiness' Emma and Mr Knightley will enjoy (484), not in order to undercut or qualify that happiness, but for another, more important reason. Part of Austen's intention in *Emma* is to render irritating characters like Mrs Elton so faithfully as to provoke her readers, and then to require that the reader accept them, and sometimes love them, because he knows them so well. Mr Knightley gives almost a formula for the novel when he says to Emma, 'I could not think about you so much without doating on you, faults and all' (462). While the reader is not quite asked to dote on Mrs Elton, faults and all, he must allow his intimate knowledge of her to be felt more strongly than his irritation and annoyance. Her comment on the marriage, for example ('Very little white satin, very few lace veils; a most pitiful business! – Selina would stare when she heard of it'), perfectly accords with everything the reader knows of her: her love of finery and parade, and her self-complacency on the score of her relation to Selina Suckling and the barouche-landau.

Austen's intentions for Mrs Elton are best understood by comparison with her treatment of an equally abrasive character in *Mansfield Park*, Mrs Norris. After Maria Rushworth's elopement with Henry Crawford, 'Mrs Norris ... as most attached to Maria, was really the greatest sufferer. Maria was her first favourite, the dearest of all; the match had been her own contriving, as she had been wont with such pride of heart to feel and say, and this conclusion of it almost overpowered her. She was an altered creature, quieted, stupified, indifferent to every thing that passed' (448). Mrs Norris is humiliated as Mrs Elton is not. The alteration in her creates some slight sympathy in the reader as an accompaniment to his sense that she has got just what she deserves – more sympathy, certainly, than he would have supposed possible. Having done this, Austen allows her removal from Mansfield to be a welcome relief to the other characters. 'Not even Fanny had tears for aunt Norris – not even when she was gone for ever' (466). Sir Thomas's response is even more significant:

> He had felt her as an hourly evil, which was so much the worse, as there seemed no chance of its ceasing but with life; she seemed a part of himself, that must be borne for ever. To be relieved from her, therefore, was so great a felicity, that had she not left bitter re-membrances behind her, there might have been danger of his learning almost to approve the evil which produced such a good (465–6).

What Fanny has considered 'the little irritations, sometimes introduced by aunt Norris' (392) are wholly eliminated from the world *Mansfield Park* creates at the end. Mrs Elton, on the other hand, is the world. Neither she nor the irritations and annoyances she creates are eliminated from Highbury. She cannot be expelled, so she must be known, accepted and absorbed.

Emma is a comedy more of intimacy than of judgment, though judgment of character is so frequently at issue in the novel and though the plot is brilliantly constructed to challenge and exercise the reader's judgment. Because intimacy is the special intention of *Emma*, it dictates many details of composition, including the need to portray a close, small world like Highbury faithfully and exhaustively. The society of Highbury, its amusements, its interests, its daily routines, must all be made familiar to the reader. Most important is the need to make characters known, and Austen fulfils this need through conversations in which the characters make themselves known as they discuss themselves or others. These conversations are enormously complex as a result. No analysis can exhaust the implications or connections of even the briefest of them, for everything in *Emma* reflects on everything else. The novel presents readers with a perfectly smooth, taut, rounded surface; its integrity is like that of a sphere, offering criticism no handles. Nevertheless, some of the techniques which allow Austen to create a world of such fullness and intricacy are visible in the conversation from the early chapter in which Mr Knightley and Mrs Weston discuss Emma.

The most important of these techniques is simple and direct: Austen promotes intimacy between her readers and her characters by creating characters who are intimate with each other and whose speech reflects their intimacy. Mr Knightley and Mrs Weston know Emma well, and what they say of her reflects both their affection and their knowledge of her, faults and all. They also know each other so well that earlier in the scene they can openly discuss what might seem an impossibly rude, threatening or painful subject: Mr Knightley's disapproval of Mrs Weston as a governess for Emma. Mrs Weston says, most directly, 'I am sure you always thought me unfit for the office I held,' and Mr Knightley's reply is even more direct. ' "Yes," said he, smiling. "You are better placed *here*; very fit for a wife, but not at all for a governess" ' (38). Mr Knightley's smile indicates the affectionate intimacy that saves his remark from harshness, and Mrs Weston is not at all offended. That their intimacy is perfectly reciprocal is clear when Mrs Weston corrects him later in the scene and he accepts her correction with good grace. She advises him not to discuss with Mr John Knightley or Isabella his disapproval of Emma's 'intimacy' with Harriet Smith, as she does not 'think any possible good' will be achieved. She continues,

'It has been so many years my province to give advice, that you cannot be surprized, Mr Knightley, at this little remains of office.'

'Not at all,' cried he; 'I am much obliged to you for it. It is very good advice, and it shall have a better fate than your advice has often found; for it shall be attended to.'

'Mrs John Knightley is easily alarmed, and might be made unhappy about her sister.'

'Be satisfied,' said he, 'I will not raise any outcry. I will keep my ill-humour to myself. I have a very sincere interest in Emma. Isabella does not seem more my sister; has never excited a greater interest; perhaps hardly so great. There is an anxiety, a curiosity in what one feels for Emma. I wonder what will become of her!'

'So do I,' said Mrs Weston gently; 'very much.'

'She always declares she will never marry, which, of course, means just nothing at all. But I have no idea that she has yet ever seen a man she cared for. It would not be a bad thing for her to be very much in love with a proper object. I should like to see Emma in love, and in some doubt of a return; it would do her good. But there is nobody hereabouts to attach her; and she goes so seldom from home' (40-1).

This passage, brief as it is and simple by comparison to any exchange in which Emma herself participates, bears an ironic relation to almost all of the plot. Mr Knightley is not yet aware of his own love for Emma, and when she later shows an interest in Frank Churchill even before meeting him, Mr Knightley's hostility and jealousy reveal to himself his love for her. 'He had been in love with Emma, and jealous of Frank Churchill, from about the same period, one sentiment having probably enlightened him as to the other' (432). So far from liking 'to see Emma in love, and in some doubt of a return', when he suspects 'a something of private liking, of private understanding even, between Frank Churchill and Jane' (344), a liking that would threaten Emma if she loves Frank, he attempts to warn her, for 'He could not see her in a situation of such danger, without trying to preserve her' (349). More ironic still, when Emma actually is in love with a proper object (Mr Knightley himself), and in some doubt of a return, it *does* do her good, for it makes her 'understand the deceptions she had been thus practising on herself, and living under! – The blunders, the blindness of her own head and heart!' (411-2).

A kind of linear irony is at work here, although the term seems increasingly inadequate for the connections between this passage and others in the novel. Linear irony implies reversal, which does not really describe what happens between Mr Knightley's ambiguously phrased declaration that 'Isabella does not seem more my sister' and his later very moving response when Emma invites him to dance, saying, 'You have shown that you can dance, and you know we are not really so much brother and sister as to make it at all improper.' 'Brother and sister! no, indeed' (331). This exchange is highly charged with feeling because of the incongruity between Mr Knightley's now conscious love for Emma and her still unconscious love for him. His denial of a fraternal relation to her reflects back on his earlier remark poignantly rather than ironically or comically. The reader should note too that Emma's words here are phrased ambiguously, quite like his earlier ones. Even when both are unaware of their love, they are far from ready to see themselves as brother and sister.

A less powerful connection but an important one exists also between Mr Knightley's willingness to keep his ill-humour to himself and such incidents as Emma's readiness to repress her discontent when Mr Weston injudiciously invites Mrs Elton to join their expedition to Box Hill:

> so it was to be, if she had no objection. Now, as her objection was nothing but her very great dislike of Mrs Elton, of which Mr Weston must already be perfectly aware, it was not worth bringing forward again: – it could not be done without a reproof to him, which would be giving pain to his wife; and she found herself therefore obliged to consent to an arrangement which she would have done a great deal to avoid; an arrangement which would probably expose her even to the degradation of being said to be of Mrs Elton's party! Every feeling was offended; and the forbearance of her outward submission left a heavy arrear due of secret severity in her reflections on the unmanageable good-will of Mr Weston's temper (353).

Touches like these make *Emma* the miracle it is. The complexity of response required of a reader is immense. He must register Emma's faults and virtues at every line, for her snobbery and her consideration are perfectly intermixed. The reader also, sharing Emma's hearty dislike of Mrs Elton, will be equally indignant at Mr Weston's 'unmanageable good-will', and is as likely as Emma to wish some outlet for this indignation. But annoyance, irritation, ill-humour and indignation are not allowed free expression: they must not be permitted to hurt others. Forbearance is, therefore, of great value in this novel, although not the greatest. Emma's forbearance here is admirable, and does make one love her. In this scene, however, she is forbearing, not loving or good-natured, and forbearance can give way under stress, as Emma's does at Box Hill, allowing her to insult Miss Bates. Love, a higher and more generous sentiment, is required. Emma's love for her father, who is a clear foil to Miss Bates, makes forbearance unnecessary or irrelevant in her relations with him, although his demands on her are ceaseless and his selfish fretfulness far more irritating than Miss Bates's verbosity. Mr Knightley's readiness to suppress his ill-humour in the early scene thus announces a theme which will be sounded and varied again and again in

Emma, reaching a climax at Box Hill. Similarly, his ready acceptance of advice echoes another important motif, for giving and taking advice are frequently at issue, whether Emma is advising Harriet or being advised by Mr Knightley.

Austen uses the dialogue between Mr Knightley and Mrs Weston to create other, more immediate effects on the reader than linear irony allows. One such effect is produced when Mr Knightley declares that 'there is nobody hereabouts to attach' Emma. His comments on her in all of Chapter V ostensibly declare him an affectionate friend with no other idea in mind. He considers that she has never yet seen anyone she could care for. Austen guards against the reader's anticipating the conclusion too soon by allowing Mr Knightley thus to ignore the possibility that he could be Emma's suitor; the reader is made more likely to ignore it also. Yet Mr Knightley's ignorance is no unfair trick to mislead the reader. His unconscious love for Emma is not merely necessary to the plot but perfectly consistent with the history of his relation to her. When Mr Knightley claims, on the other hand, that 'There is an anxiety, a curiosity in what one feels for Emma. I wonder what will become of her,' Austen's intentions are different. She is allowing him to articulate the central issue of the novel. What one feels for Emma is as important, page by page, as the unfolding of her character and destiny, and Austen is using Mr Knightley's speech in the simplest, most direct way to guide the reader's attention to the question of his own response to Emma. The speeches of Mr Knightley and Mrs Weston also, in an unobtrusive way, give some information about Emma's early history, which helps the reader to understand, allow for and feel for her character, particularly the information that 'ever since she was twelve, Emma has been mistress of the house and of you all' (37). What Mr Knightley and Mrs Weston say also has other effects on the reader's response to Emma. Their speeches voice their different estimations of her character and conduct (especially of her intimacy with Harriet Smith) and require the reader to judge between them. This use of conversation is, however, more conventional and less daring than its use as a kind of aside to the reader, reminding him of his task. Mr Knightley's mentioning 'an anxiety, a curiosity' in one's feelings for Emma is rather like Edmund Bertram's declaring to Fanny that 'There is no reason in the world why you should not be important where you are known' (26). Both statements are addressed to the reader as much as to Mrs Weston or Fanny.

The effects any passage in *Emma* has upon a reader's perceptions and judgments are difficult to separate from both emotional and comic effects. Techniques and their effects are much less obvious than in *Pride and*

Prejudice: what is the effect, for instance, on a second reading, of Mr Knightley's ignorance of his own heart in Chapter V? Some amusement is certainly felt at the discrepancy between this ignorance and his decided, definite pronouncements about his feelings for Emma and indeed about everything else. Yet this amusement is qualified; his ignorance comes to seem painful, as it leads to his difficult position as observer of Emma's flirtation with Frank Churchill. Thus, his response to Mrs Weston's praise of Emma's beauty creates an almost indefinable effect. He says first, 'I confess that I have seldom seen a face or figure more pleasing to me than her's. But I am a partial old friend,' and then more powerfully, 'I love to look at her' (39). The incongruity between what he acknowledges to himself and what he really feels, between so much open and so much concealed affection, is intensely moving. Certainly the effect is not like that produced when Elizabeth Bennet tells Darcy, 'It is particularly incumbent on those who never change their opinion, to be secure of judging properly at first' (93), even though Elizabeth's remark is not purely comic either. The different effects seem attributable to the higher emotional content which informs and underlies dialogue in the later novels. Unacknowledged or suppressed love is a major theme in them all, along with an investigatioin of its consequences.

Concealment in general is also prominent in *Emma*. Mrs Weston's reply to Mr Knightley's comments about wishing to see Emma in love is oblique, for 'Part of her meaning was to conceal some favourite thoughts of her own and Mr Weston's on the subject, as much as possible. There were wishes at Randalls respecting Emma's destiny, but it was not desirable to have them suspected' (41). These thoughts are of a marriage between Frank Churchill and Emma, thoughts Emma herself entertains. It is typical of Austen's practice in *Emma* that she should end this scene, which has expressed so much openness, good will and intimacy, with some slight obliquity and reserve. As Austen comments later, when Emma has received Mr Knightley's declaration of love, and is obliged to conceal both her former fear that he loved Harriet, and Harriet's existing attachment, 'Seldom, very seldom, does complete truth belong to any human disclosure; seldom can it happen that something is not a little disguised, or a little mistaken; but where, as in this case, though the conduct is mistaken, the feelings are not, it may not be very material' (431).

This passage has been sometimes taken as evidence that Austen acknowledges an almost modern consciousness of human isolation and of the impossibility of knowing or being known. On the contrary: the whole thrust of *Emma* is toward openness, knowledge and intimacy. The

limits or restrictions which human nature dictates for these qualities
(limits the novels fully concede) are less interesting to Austen than are
their possibilities in human relations. Once Emma hears that Harriet is
engaged to Robert Martin,

> High in the rank of her most serious and heartfelt felicities, was the
> reflection that all necessity of concealment from Mr Knightley would
> soon be over. The disguise, equivocation, mystery, so hateful to her to
> practise, might soon be over. She could now look forward to giving
> him that full and perfect confidence which her disposition was most
> ready to welcome as a duty (475).

This passage carries more weight within *Emma* than its counterpart,
reinforced as it is by the very moving, open, intimate conversations
between Mr Knightley and Emma after their engagement.

The plot of *Emma* moves toward the release and acknowledgement of
concealed love, and the result is intimacy. The secret engagement of Jane
Fairfax and Frank Churchill is revealed and all the mystification associated
with it dispelled, just as the unconscious love of Emma and Mr Knightley
is made conscious. In the process the plot takes in a great deal more,
including Emma's misconduct, her various stages of repentance, and her
relapses, all of which have complicated effects in controlling the reader's
judgment of her and sympathy for her. Yet the emphasis on judgment,
enhanced as it is by the central mystery tantalizingly presented for the
reader to make out, is oddly undercut at the end, making *Emma* the
comedy of intimacy that it is, not a comedy of judgment.

Frank Churchill, for example, has conducted himself in the novel so as
to invite and deserve the reader's harshest criticism. He too parodies
Emma's worst qualities, for he fools and manipulates everyone. Emma says
to him at last, 'I think there is a little likeness between us' (478), but in
fact Frank is much worse than Emma. He is irresponsible and thoughtless. He torments Jane, whom he loves. When his duplicity and cruelty
are first revealed, Emma's righteous indignation is most welcome to the
reader and voices his own judgment of Frank's conduct: 'Impropriety!
Oh! Mrs Weston – it is too calm a censure. Much, much beyond
impropriety! – It has sunk him, I cannot say how it has sunk him in my
opinion. So unlike what a man should be! – None of that upright
integrity, that strict adherence to truth and principle, that disdain of trick
and littleness, which a man should display in every transaction of his life'
(397). Emma is, of course, thinking unconsciously of Mr Knightley as she
speaks, and a little of her own impropriety in suspecting an attachment

between Jane and Mr Dixon and then in imparting that suspicion to Frank. Every judgment in *Emma* is qualified by self-regarding consideration like these. Nevertheless, Emma's indignation is meant to be felt as the first in a series of judgments of Frank Churchill's character, judgments whose reversals undercut moral judgment in general and Emma's, Mr Knightley's and the reader's in particular.

Emma herself is soon forced by Mrs Weston to 'listen better' to excuses for Frank, and is in any case quickly taken up with her own concerns (thinking Frank's uncle would have consented as readily to a marriage with Harriet as with Jane). The summary of Mr Knightley's response to Frank's engagement offers an even finer and more sustained joke on moral judgment than does the course of Emma's first response: 'He had found [Emma] agitated and low. – Frank Churchill was a villain. – He heard her declare that she had never loved him. Frank Churchill's character was not desperate. – She was his own Emma, by hand and word, when they returned into the house; and if he could have thought of Frank Churchill then, he might have deemed him a very good sort of fellow' (433). This response finds an echo in Emma's later reaction to Frank Churchill's letter of explanation: 'though it was impossible not to feel that he had been wrong, yet he had been less wrong than she had supposed – and he had suffered, and was very sorry – and he was so grateful to Mrs Weston, and so much in love with Miss Fairfax, and she was so happy herself, that there was no being severe; and could he have entered the room, she must have shaken hands with him as heartily as ever' (444). This letter has much the same softening effect on the reader as on Emma, and so Mr Knightley is brought back again to provide one more reversal as he goes over it, revealing in his stringent comments what the reader and Emma should have thought. And yet Mr Knightley's heart is hardly in the subject. He doesn't want to read the letter in the first place, cuts short his judgment, and proceeds to talk with Emma of their marriage: 'I have another person's interest at present so much at heart, that I cannot think any longer about Frank Churchill' (448).

The didactic effect of *Emma* is a complicated one. The reader's judgment is evoked, beguiled, confounded, refined and then dissolved or transcended by love. Even more is required of his sympathies. Miss Bates, for example, is so perfectly rendered in her tiresome verbosity that Walter Scott's review cites Austen's treatment as a fault: 'Characters of folly or simplicity, such as those of old Woodhouse and Miss Bates, are ridiculous when first presented, but if too often brought forward or too long dwelt upon, their prosing is apt to become as tiresome in fiction as in real society.'[3] Yet Scott's reaction half fulfils Austen's intention. Unless Miss

Bates is felt as boring, even irritating, and unless the reader is to that extent implicated in Emma's insult at Box Hill, one part of the effect of that splendid scene is lost.

At Box Hill, all the sexual and social tension, irritation and frustration that the action has generated explodes. The reader is made to know what every character is feeling during the scene partly through dialogue and narrative, and partly through the knowledge of each that the novel has so carefully imparted. The amount and kind of bad feeling expressed, the incongruity between every character's feelings and motives, the various ways in which each partly understands and partly mistakes the others, are all astonishing. Emma's much-cited insult to Miss Bates is not surprising in the context of so much bad feeling, and yet it is shocking. Almost as shocking is Mr Weston's conundrum, which immediately follows: 'What two letters of the alphabet are there, that express perfection? . . . M. and A. – Em – ma. – Do you understand?' (371). The juxtaposition of Emma's most unkind act and Mr Weston's tribute is a touch typical of *Emma*. Yet the scene does not stop here, as in a sense it should; it keeps going, and the reader's attention is absorbed by the ugliness which follows, most notably Frank Churchill's declaration to Emma that when he returns from abroad, 'I shall come to you for my wife' (373), a flirtatious remark aimed at Jane Fairfax that seems to her to be serious courtship of Emma, and to Emma a 'commission' to groom Harriet for the post, for deluded as she is otherwise, Emma does know that Frank Churchill's gallantry to her 'now, in her own estimation, meant nothing' (368). Indeed, the reader would be in as much danger as Emma of overlooking her rudeness without Mr Knightley's rebuke. His words to Emma, 'How could you be so unfeeling,' are addressed in part to the reader, and indeed his words so firmly fix the incident as the central one of the scene, both in Emma's mind and in the reader's, that to reread the chapter and to find Emma's insult buried in so much more obviously ugly interaction is a shock. That Emma is struck and chastened by Mr Knightley's rebuke is clear, not only in the tears she sheds going home, but in her reflections in the evening. 'As a daughter, she hoped she was not without a heart. She hoped no one could have said to her, "How could you be so unfeeling to your father?" '(377). To be 'feeling' in the best sense is what *Emma* teaches, and complicated sequences like these account for its extraordinary power to evoke, exasperate, perplex, extend and enlarge the reader's capacity to feel. Austen's attempts to educate the reader's sympathies as well as his judgments have never been so ambitious or so successful.

*   *   *

Persuasion is very different. Although Austen's abiding concern with the interrelations of feeling and judgment are responsible for a good deal of continuity in her works, considerable diversity arises from the perfecting of her techniques and the extending of her range. Between *Emma* and *Persuasion*, however, a disparity exists which may seem to indicate regression rather than extension. The elegaic tone of *Persuasion* may appear thin after the energy of *Emma*. As D.F. Tovey has rightly noted, however, 'When an artist is great enough to produce a number of works widely differing in character, there is nothing he enjoys so much as the strongest possible contrasts between two successive works'. He adduces the 'unique sense of power' an artist will feel when 'he finds himself fit for a delicate task just after he has triumphed in a colossal one'.[4] These words could be a formula for the composition of *Persuasion*. The restrained yet poignant tone is highly appropriate to a story whose heroine is no longer young and has made her significant moral choice, to break her engagement, seven years before the novel opens. The emotional costs and consequences of this choice, and of being 'forced into prudence' (30) are the subject, along with the possibility of escaping those consequences so as to have a second chance for youth and happiness.

The differences between *Persuasion* and the other two late novels are more interesting than their similarities. The emotional content of *Persuasion* is very high, quite as high as in *Mansfield Park* or *Emma*, but emotional interest is not as widely dispersed among the characters. Anne's feelings are registered almost to the exclusion of anyone else's, and more important, her feelings are seldom expressed in dialogue. Not conversation but silent attentiveness is Anne Elliot's most characteristic mode of expressing herself for much of the novel, thereby giving great power to her exchange with Captain Harville at the end. Her reserve breaks down far enough that she speaks her own feelings at last: ' "All the privilege I claim for my own sex (it is not a very enviable one, you need not covet it) is that of loving longest, when existence or when hope is gone." She could not immediately have uttered another sentence; her heart was too full, her breath too much oppressed' (235). Although Anne unmistakably expresses the strength of her feelings in this scene, she stops short of complete openness. Only Captain Wentworth, listening nearby, understands the meaning behind her words and their relation to her own experience.

The techniques of *Persuasion* do not differ entirely from those of the preceding novels. Dialogue does have importance, and Austen does incorporate some linear irony into its structure, for this scene between Anne and Captain Harville, overheard by Wentworth, reverses an earlier, often-quoted one in which Anne overhears Wentworth talking to Louisa Musgrove, ostensibly of his impressions of Louisa's firmness of character, but actually about his judgment of Anne's weakness. Again, only Anne can infer the direction of his thoughts from his words. He concludes, in 'his former earnest tone',

'My first wish for all, whom I am interested in, is that they should be firm. If Louisa Musgrove would be beautiful and happy in her November of life, she will cherish all her present powers of mind.'

He had done, – and was unanswered. It would have surprised Anne, if Louisa could have readily answered such a speech – words of such interest, spoken with such serious warmth! – she could imagine what Louisa was feeling. For herself – she feared to move, lest she should be seen. While she remained, a bush of low rambling holly protected her, and they were moving on. Before they were beyond her hearing, however, Louisa spoke again.

'Mary is good-natured enough in many respects,' said she; 'but she does sometimes provoke me excessively, by her nonsense and her pride; the Elliot pride. She has a great deal too much of the Elliot pride. – We do so wish that Charles had married Anne instead. – I suppose you know he wanted to marry Anne?'

After a moment's pause, Captain Wentworth said,

'Do you mean that she refused him?'

'Oh! yes, certainly.'

'When did that happen?'

'I do not exactly know, for Henrietta and I were at school at the time; but I believe about a year before he married Mary. I wish she had accepted him. We should all have liked her a great deal better; and papa and mamma always think it was her great friend Lady Russell's doing, that she did not. – They think Charles might not be learned and bookish enough to please Lady Russell, and that therefore, she persuaded Anne to refuse him.'

The sounds were retreating, and Anne distinguished no more. Her own emotions still kept her fixed. She had much to recover from, before she could move. The listener's proverbial fate was not absolutely hers; she had heard no evil of herself, – but she had heard a great deal of very painful import. She saw how her own character was considered by Captain Wentworth; and there had been just that degree of feeling and curiosity about her in his manner, which must give her extreme agitation (88–9).

This passage underscores the major difference in technique between *Persuasion* and *Mansfield Park* or *Emma*. The speeches of Wentworth and Louisa actually have less effect on the reader than the narrative passages which describe Anne's responses to their dialogue. In this sense, narrative is more important than dialogue throughout *Persuasion*. Austen's principal interest in this passage is to convey Anne's feelings to the reader, not Wentworth's or Louisa's. The narrative focuses on Anne's feelings, yet what is left unsaid about them is more important than what is said. Anne's feelings in hearing what she supposes to be Wentworth's courtship of Louisa must be inferred, for they are not precisely stated. Instead, the narrative dwells on the emotion she projects onto Louisa: 'she could imagine what Louisa was feeling'. But neither Louisa's feelings nor Anne's are really specified. 'For herself – she feared to move, lest she should be seen'; 'Her own emotions still kept her fixed'; 'She had much to recover from'; 'she had heard a great deal of very painful import'; 'there had been just that degree of feeling and curiosity about her in his manner, which must give her extreme agitation.' Fear, pain and agitation are mentioned, but their precise direction and content are left to the reader's imaginative sympathy, particularly with respect to the laconic 'For herself'. Anne's sensations at hearing Louisa speak so casually of her marrying Charles Musgrove or at hearing Louisa attribute her refusing him to Lady Russell's interference must also be imagined in relation to details we have been given earlier: that Lady Russell persuaded Anne to break her engagement to Captain Wentworth, and that she would have liked to persuade Anne to marry Charles Musgrove.

Anne's feelings in these circumstances are readily imagined and felt, but would be registered differently and less immediately by the reader if the narrative spelled them out more precisely. Although Austen's dialogue often operates in the way narrative does in this passage, frequently requiring much imaginative effort from the reader's sympathies and judgment if he is to take in all that is happening, the narrative seldom requires this much direct engagement. Comparison with *Mansfield Park* nicely illustrates the difference. Fanny Price and Anne Elliot resemble each other, as many critics have noted, in their forced reserve, their isolation, their goodness and their position: watching the man they love court another woman. Nevertheless, although the narrative of *Mansfield Park* often registers Fanny's pain, the effect produced is not the same, whether Austen chooses to describe her feelings closely and specifically or not. When Fanny watches Mary Crawford and Edmund rehearse a love scene from *Lovers' Vows*, 'In watching them she forgot herself; and agitated by the increasing spirit of Edmund's manner, had once closed the page and turned away exactly as he wanted help. It was imputed to very reasonable weariness, and she was thanked and pitied; but she deserved their pity, more than she hoped they would ever surmise' (170). A general awareness of Fanny's painful feelings is possible, but nothing more, as in *Mansfield Park* interest is distributed more generally among the characters. The reader is made almost as interested in and aware of the feelings of Edmund and Mary as of Fanny in this sequence. When, on the other hand, Fanny is alone after having displeased Sir Thomas by her refusal of Henry Crawford, the spelling out of her distress, while poignant enough, is not as painful as reading Sir Thomas's angry rebuke and does not call for the same effort of imagination:

> Her mind was all disorder. The past, present, future, every thing was terrible. But her uncle's anger gave her the severest pain of all. Selfish and ungrateful! to have appeared so to him! She was miserable for ever. She had no one to take her part, to counsel, or speak for her. Her only friend was absent. He might have softened his father; but all, perhaps all, would think her selfish and ungrateful. She might have to endure the reproach again and again; she might hear it, or see it, or know it to exist for ever in every connection about her. She could not but feel some resentment against Mr Crawford; yet, if he really loved her, and were unhappy too! – it was all wretchedness together (321).

A little distance from Fanny is required by such phrases as 'She was miserable for ever'. Her immature certainty that present pain will endure always is dwelt on in the passage and distances the reader slightly from that pain, although it is very real. On the other hand, very little emotional distance from Anne Elliot is permitted to the reader of *Persuasion*.

In *Mansfield Park* and *Emma*, Austen masters techniques which allow her to render dense, highly-complicated worlds with a number of important central characters. Fanny Price and Emma Woodhouse are the most central, certainly, but the claims of other characters are powerfully registered. In *Persuasion*, everything centres on Anne Elliot. Other characters are important insofar as they either draw her out or suppress her, as her father and Elizabeth do: she 'was nobody with either' (5). Once she leaves Kellynch, however, all the other characters draw her out to some extent, even Mary, the most selfish of them, for Anne always can involve herself imaginatively in others' concerns, although others seldom respond in kind. The other characters are, indeed, largely rendered to the reader through Anne's imaginative involvement with them. As a result, the world of *Persuasion* is attenuated, very deliberately. Thus, although examples of nearly all the literary techniques Austen has developed can be found, they are employed sparingly. Parallels and contrasts among the characters do exist, for instance, and are implied when Louisa Musgrove mentions the Elliot pride. The coldness, reserve and pride of the Elliots are explicitly opposed to the cheerfulness of the Musgroves and the warmth and openness of the naval characters. Similarly, the dialogue between Louisa and Captain Wentworth has some ironic relations to the plot. Anne's reflections on Louisa's accident at Lyme refer to this earlier exchange: 'Anne wondered whether it ever occured to him now, to question the justness of his own previous opinion as to the universal felicity and advantage of firmness of character' (116). The indications given in the exchange of Wentworth's 'feeling and curiosity' about Anne are significant too, as his misjudgment of her is important, and as the reader shares much of Anne's concern to probe his feelings. But the major effect of this or any other exchange is to make the reader feel for Anne.

Austen's interest in educating judgment and sympathy is confined in *Persuasion* to what she wants her readers to feel for Anne. Furthermore, Austen has set moral conflict and moral choice to one side in this novel. The conventional conflict between love (for Captain Wentworth) and duty (to Lady Russell), a conflict which provides the stuff of so many third-rate plays and novels, and vitiates better novels like *Cecilia* and *Sir Charles Grandison*, is set nearly eight years in the past. Although Anne makes several references to this conflict, regretting her choice at the start of the novel and, very naturally, justifying it to herself at the end once she has regained Wentworth's love, Austen is not really interested in the question of whether Anne's choice was right. Instead, Austen interests herself in the emotional consequences of such a choice. Anne's sufferings as a result of having been 'forced into prudence' in her youth are not dwelt on, but the results are clear: 'Her attachment and regrets had, for a long time, clouded every enjoyment of youth; and an early loss of bloom and spirits had been their lasting effect' (28).

The subject of *Persuasion* is Anne's recovery of youth, bloom, sexual attraction and more: the delivery of her emotional life from the contracting effects of loss. Anne recovers all she has lost. The plot releases her by bringing her into contact with different sets of people who allow her to open herself a bit. Each new set permits Anne to experience and to express more and more feeling. As her world expands, from Kellynch to Uppercross, Lyme, and Bath, so does her emotional life. All the later novels are expansive in a sense, for their power to create cumulative effects means that their worlds grow larger with meaning as the stories progress. In *Persuasion*, however, this effect is confined to the opening out of Anne's feelings. This structure, simple and obvious by comparison with the structures of the novels that precede it, allows the subject matter of *Persuasion* to be Anne's gradual recovery of possibility, of hope and finally of happiness. Openness and love replace restraint and loss. Although they could scarcely be more different from those of *Emma*, the theme and treatment in *Persuasion* are lovely in themselves.

Evidence that *Persuasion* represents variation and extension of Austen's powers rather than relaxation is offered by *Sanditon*, the novel left incomplete at her death. Its twelve chapters form an exposition which barely suffices to sketch the characters and themes and fails to hint at the development they will receive, yet the chapters create a world as full and varied as that of *Persuasion* is purposely attenuated. The village of Sanditon and its activities are presented in minute detail which exceeds the portrait of Highbury in *Emma*. The sensible judgments of Charlotte Heywood are slightly touched by a literary imagination and are counterpointed with variously deformed judgments: the hasty and hazardous speculations of Mr Parker, the selfish and mercenary calculations of Lady Denham, the hypochondria of Mr Parker's sisters and brother, the literary libertinism of Sir Edward Denham. As Charlotte points out, 'The Parkers, were no doubt a family of Imagination & quick feelings' (*MW*, p. 412), and clearly the interaction of these qualities with judgment would have been a major theme. Southam has called attention to the enigmatic quality events and characters take on when seen through Charlotte's eyes, and to her difficulty in judging them; he notes that the enigma confronts the reader also: 'Jane Austen is being purposely enigmatic, challenging us to fathom the importance of the characters and the direction of the plot'.[5] If so, she has assimilated the burlesque energy of *Northanger Abbey* (its playful attempts to jolt the reader's expectations, and its jokes on the relation of literature and life) to subject matter typical of the later novels: registering and requiring judgment at every point while perplexing it and indicating the fallibilities and absurdities which result from its interaction with feeling or imagination.

The fragment ends with the entrance of Sidney Parker, a character who is clearly to be as sensible and as perceptive as Charlotte, whatever his other qualities. His presence, added to Clara Brereton's and Charlotte's, would have allowed the novel to begin in earnest, for he offers the possibility of flirtation or courtship and, more important, of sensible conversation: in an Austen novel, at least three sensible characters distributed among the dullards and fools are required for that. Conversation in this sense is all that *Sanditon* lacks to make it promise as much as *Emma*. But it is vain to regret the Austen novels we lack, while we have the rest.

Austen's desire to educate the judgment and sympathy of readers encourages her to develop increasingly sophisticated and effective methods for realizing her intentions. Awareness of these didactic intentions helps in turn to define her achievement. Attention to the ways in which she manipulates the perceptions, judgment and feelings of her readers makes it impossible to feel the presence of limits in any of the novels after *Northanger Abbey*, so convincing and absorbing are they and so close are their concerns to the ordinary concerns of daily life: forming impressions of people, modulating them as closer relations are established, and producing those adjustments and compromises between the pressures and demands of others' personalities and one's own which are required to sustain affection and intimacy in the relations one already has. In Austen's novels, the concerns of literature and of everyday life are one, and in *Emma* they receive their fullest and most powerful treatment: using a highly formal structure, the novel creates an almost impenetrable density which is, I think, as close as art can come to rendering the formless density of life.

Notes and References

INTRODUCTION

1. 'Jane Austen at Sixty', *Nation*, 15 December 1923, p. 433; rpt in Ian Watt (ed.), *Jane Austen: A Collection of Critical Essays* (Englewood Cliffs, NJ, 1963) p. 15. (Hereafter cited as *Critical Essays*.)
2. I am indebted to Southam's 'Introduction' in B.C. Southam (ed.), *Jane Austen: The Critical Heritage* (London, 1968; hereafter cited as *Critical Heritage*) for this useful distinction between nineteenth- and twentieth-century Austen criticism (p. 32). The study of Austen's artistic development is slightly perplexed by the difficult question of when her early novels were actually written. In my own study, I accept a dating based largely on the order of publication. I consider that *Northanger Abbey* (completed 1803; published 1818) represents Austen's earliest work, *Sense and Sensibility* (published 1811) her first mature novel, and *Pride and Prejudice* (1813) her latest and finest early work. I see a complex but coherent artistic development in these novels as we have them, that is, presumably revised just before publication (except for *Northanger Abbey*, published posthumously), although the earlier versions of all three novels were written in an entirely different order, according to Cassandra Austen's memorandum:

   > First Impressions begun in Oct 1796
   > Finished in Augt 1797. Published
   > afterwards, with alterations & contractions
   > under the Title of Pride & Prejudice.
   > Sense & Sensibility begun Nov. 1797
   > I am sure that something of the
   > same story & characters had been
   > written earlier & called Elinor & Marianne
   >
   > North-hanger Abbey was written
   > about the years 98 & 99

   (The memorandum is printed by Southam, *Jane Austen's Literary Manuscripts* [Oxford, 1964] p. 53.)
3. The phrase and the notion are Mark Schorer's in 'The Humiliation of Emma Woodhouse', *Literary Review*, Summer 1959; rpt in David Lodge (ed.), *Jane Austen: Emma, A Casebook* (London, 1968) p. 177. (Hereafter cited as *Casebook*.)
4. Those who see Austen as a 'subversive' critic of her world (Schorer, D. W. Harding, Marvin Mudrick) belong in this group, as do a few of the critics who explicitly reject this reading, among them Andrew Wright and Lionel Trilling. The latter also locate Austen's triumph in her irony, but define it differently. For example, although Trilling refutes the criticisms which *Mansfield Park* has received for its negative treatment of the witty and ironic Crawfords, he does so by claiming for the novel a

higher kind of irony: 'an irony directed against irony itself' ('*Mansfield Park,*' *The Opposing Self* [New York, 1955]; rpt in *Critical Essays*, p. 135).

5. See Susan Morgan's *In the Meantime: Character and Perception in Jane Austen's Novels* (Chicago, 1980); two important studies which place Austen in an eighteenth-century context are Alastair Duckworth's *The Improvement of the Estate* (Baltimore, 1971) and Marilyn Butler's *Jane Austen and the War of Ideas* (Oxford, 1975).

6. 'Introduction' to *Critical Essays,*, p. 12.

7. Stuart M. Tave, *Some Words of Jane Austen* (Chicago, 1973) p. 34.

8. A few examples will suffice. Richard Simpson speaks of the 'didactic purpose and even nomenclature of her novels' (*North British Review*, 52 [1890]; rpt in *Critical Heritage*, p. 244). For him, Austen didactically and habitually exalts 'judgment over passion' (p. 245). Richard Whately discusses didacticism more thoroughly, echoing the well-known arguments of Henry Fielding in *Joseph Andrews* (Book I, ch. i, opening paragraphs) and Samuel Johnson in *Rambler* No. 4. Whately praises Austen's talent for making her novels probable, because this allows 'instruction in human character and conduct' to be the more efficacious: poetic justice which is brought about by improbable occurrences either encourages readers to become reckless, calculating on 'lucky incidents', or conversely, encourages readers in a sceptical attitude toward the rewards of virtuous conduct, if those rewards are so improbably achieved (*Quarterly Review*, 24 [1821]; rpt *Critical Heritage*, pp. 88, 89). His discussion limits Austen's didactic intentions to supplying 'practical good sense and instructive example' (p. 93). George Henry Lewes goes further, and approximates in part my own view, when he observes that we see into her characters' 'hearts and hopes, their motives, their struggles within themselves; and a sympathy is induced which, if extended to daily life and the world at large, would make the reader a more amiable person' (unsigned article, 'The Novels of Jane Austen', *Blackwood's Edinburgh Magazine*, 86 [1859]; rpt in *Critical Heritage*, p. 155).

9. David Lodge, *Language of Fiction* (London, 1966) p. 113.

10. To apply the terms 'judgment' and 'sympathy' to Austen's work is not new. They are implicit in Lascelles' discussion of the comic techniques. She finds that Austen's narratives are managed so as to appeal on the one hand to the 'critical faculty' and on the other to the 'sympathetic imagination' (*Jane Austen and her Art* [1939; rpt London: Oxford University Press, 1963] p. 142). Wayne Booth speaks of Austen's control of the reader's 'sympathy and judgment' in relation to Emma Woodhouse (*The Rhetoric of Fiction* [Chicago, 1961] pp. 243–56). He seems to consider that the reader will have difficulty in responding to Emma only; I think Austen delights in creating difficulties in response everywhere, in all the novels, for her method is always to tempt the reader into mistaken sympathies and judgments in order to correct them at last.

For an interesting study of the ways in which Fielding and Smollett successfully control readers' responses, see Wolfgang Iser's *The Implied Reader* (Baltimore, 1974). These novelists, however, do not significantly influence Austen.

11. Maria Edgeworth illustrates all these points perfectly in her novel *Ormond* (1817), for she actually summarizes her young hero's responses in emotion and in conduct to reading *Tom Jones* and *Sir Charles Grandison*. Her notion of readers' responses in conduct is wholly orthodox (her hero, Harry Ormond, tries to imitate the conduct he reads about, first Tom Jones's, then Sir Charles's). Her account clearly indicates that she thinks literature obtains its effects on the emotions through a reader's 'sympathy'. Tom Jones is attractive to Ormond because 'young readers readily assimilate and identify themselves with any character, the leading points of which resemble their

own, and in whose general feelings they sympathise' (*Harrington, a Tale; and Ormond, a Tale* [London, 1817], II, p. 155; note the 'modern' use of 'identify'). But what of an unfamiliar or even a distasteful character? 'At first he detested Sir Charles Grandison –he was so different from the friends he loved in real life, or the heroes he had admired in books' (II, p. 173). How can sympathy be obtained for Sir Charles? Here Edgeworth's notions of the process of reading and the possibilities of fiction are most distinct from Austen's. Edgeworth assumes the existence of a stock response, the response of one noble nature to another, and approves it: 'all noble natures are [susceptible] of sympathy with elevated sentiments, and with generous character. The character of Sir Charles Grandison, in spite of his ceremonious bowing on the hand, touched the nobler feelings of our young hero's mind, inspired him with virtuous emulation, made him ambitious to be a *gentleman* in the best and highest sense of the word' (II, pp. 173–4).

For Edgeworth the novelist's task is to educate the reader's emotions by drawing on a stock of finer feelings present already in nobler natures, though perhaps atrophied. For Austen, educating emotions means refining the unruly or insensitive responses of sensible but erring readers. Edgeworth depends almost entirely on stock responses to move or improve her readers; Austen demands always that the reader's stock responses be refined and educated.

12. J.M.S. Tompkins, *The Popular Novel in England, 1770-1800* (1932; rpt London, 1969) p. 27.
13. W. J. Bate and Albrecht B. Strauss (eds) *The Rambler, The Yale Edition of the Works of Samuel Johnson* (New Haven, Conn., 1969) III, p. 22. (This edition is cited hereafter as *Works*.)
14. This qualification is obscure and can bear other interpretations. Johnson may refer not to choice of theme or of moral purpose but to choice of character. If so, he is distinguishing between the freedom of choice typical in fictional treatments of character and the restraint imposed by the demands of historical accuracy. But if Johnson does mean in *Rambler* No. 4 to restrict novelists to portraits of 'the best examples only' in character, in his prefatory remarks to *Rambler* No. 97, he is able to acknowledge Richardson's successful didacticism with very different characters.
15. *Rambler* No. 97 (19 February 1751); *Works*, IV, p. 153.
16. Tompkins, *Popular Novel in England*, p. 70.
17. Clara Reeve, *The Progress of Romance* (1785); quoted by Tompkins, p. 75.
18. Richardson's professed reasons for not reading *Tom Jones* may, of course, be at some distance from his real motives; how much did jealousy operate, for instance, rather than virtuous distaste for a mixed character? Austen's view of the mixed character is, as one might expect, more balanced than Richardson's. A well-known passage from *Sanditon* testifies to her awareness that, with mixed characters like Lovelace in particular, an author's intentions and his readers' responses can be at variance. Sir Edward Denham

had read more sentimental Novels than agreed with him. His fancy had been early caught by all the impassioned, & most exceptionable parts of Richardsons [sic]; & such Authors as have since appeared to tread in Richardson's steps, so far as Man's determined pursuit of Woman in defiance of every opposition of feeling & convenience is concerned, had since occupied the greater part of his literary hours, & formed his Character. – With a perversity of Judgement, which must be attributed to his not having by Nature a very strong head, the Graces, the Spirit, the Sagacity,

& the Perseverance, of the Villain of the Story outweighed all his absurdities & all his Atrocities with Sir Edward. With him, such Conduct was Genius, Fire & Feeling. – It interested & inflamed him; & he was always more anxious for its Success and mourned over its Discomfitures with more Tenderness than c^d ever have been contemplated by the Authors (*MW*, p. 404).

Significantly, Austen attributes this misreading to the reader's 'perversity of Judgment' owing to 'not having by Nature a very strong head' as well as to 'exceptionable' parts in novels. She does seem to feel that such misreadings are wilful rather than involuntary, as Johnson's formulation (producing 'effects almost without the intervention of the will' [*Rambler* No. 4]) would have it.

19. The relevant passages may be found in *Diary and Letters of Madame D'Arblay, 1778–1840*, Charlotte Barrett (ed.), pref. and notes, Austin Dobson (London, 1904–5) II, pp. 72–3 and 154. (Cited hereafter as *Diary and Letters*.)
20. Lady Louisa Stuart, *Selections from her Manuscripts*, James Home (ed.) (New York, 1899) p. 235. Those readers who wish that Austen had written more will delight in this edition, particularly in the memoir of 'John, Duke of Argyll, and his Family', for although Lady Louisa Stuart does not write fiction, her prose resembles Austen's in certainty, wit, humour and charm.
21. *Diary and Letters*, II, p. 154.
22. This structural principle, or linear irony, has been remarked by other readers. Jane Nardin, for example, calls it 'delayed rhetorical irony' (*Those Elegant Decorums* [Albany, NY, 1973] p. 6) and connects it to Austen's thematic concern 'with deception and the reevaluation of more or less mistaken standards of value' (p. 4). This, she writes, forces the reader into a 'habit of reading with suspended judgment' (p. 7), so that 'all Jane Austen's novels are lessons in learning to think for ourselves' (p. 9). I see 'lessons' for the reader, however, as more central to Austen's intentions than Nardin does; and I consider that Austen exploits the technique of linear irony in order to engage and refine, not suspend, the reader's judgment.
23. Andrew Wright, *Jane Austen's Novels: A Study in Structure* (1953; rev. New York, 1961) p. 31.

CHAPTER 1: *NORTHANGER ABBEY*

1. Amusingly enough, when Austen describes the heroine's father on the first page as 'a very respectable man, though his name was Richard', she may actually be alluding to a passage from the burlesque 'History of England', one of her own juvenilia, which blandly, deflatingly describes Richard III as 'a very respectable Man' (*MW*, p. 141).
2. Augustus J. C. Hare (ed.), *The Life and Letters of Maria Edgeworth* (Boston, 1895) I, p. 260.
3. A. Walton Litz, *Jane Austen: A Study of Her Artistic Development* (New York, 1965) p. 63.
4. Kenneth Moler, *Jane Austen's Art of Allusion* (Lincoln, Neb., 1968) p. 40.
5. Austen uses this term favourably in a letter to her niece Anna, whose manuscript novel she is reading and criticizing. The context is revealing: 'I wish you could make Mrs F. talk more, but she must be difficult to manage & make entertaining, because there is so much good common sence & propriety about her that nothing can be very *broad*. Her Economy and her Ambition must not be staring' (*L*, p. 402). Austen clearly loves broad dialogue, though she restricts it carefully, and usually finds it inconsistent with

sensible characters. Interestingly, and perhaps significantly, in Catherine Morland Austen has created a character whose artlessness and naïveté do allow broad, entertaining dialogue even though Catherine possesses some degree of 'common sence & propriety'.

6. Kenneth Moler, *Art of Allusion*, p. 23.
7. A. Walton Litz, *Artistic Development*, p. 63.
8. For an alternative and very ingenious reading of Austen's didactic intentions, see Eric Rothstein's 'The Lessons of *Northanger Abbey*', *UTQ*, 44 (1974) pp. 14–30.
9. J. M. S. Tompkins, *Popular Novel in England*, p. 103.
10. Ann Radcliffe, *The Romance of the Forest* (London, 1971) II, p. 13. This passage is included in the selections printed by Chapman (*P*, p. 290).
11. *Romance of the Forest*, II, pp. 14–15. This passage is reprinted by Chapman only in part. It should be noted that in citing passages from this novel only, I do Radcliffe seeming injustice, as it is an early work. But even in *Udolpho* the climactic passages (Emily's discovery of what lies behind the black veil, her visit to the tower with Barnardine and near abduction by him) are not written with anything approaching Austen's skill or effectiveness.
12. Eaton Stannard Barrett, *The Heroine, or Adventures of Cherubina*, 2nd ed., rev. (London, 1814) II, pp. 137–8). Amazingly enough, the passage cited is one of Barrett's more successful ones.
13. Marvin Mudrick, *Jane Austen: Irony as Defense and Discovery* (1952; rpt Berkeley, 1968) pp. 55 and 56.
14. V. H. Hjelmaa is writing a doctoral thesis at the University of Newcastle-upon-Tyne which documents the extent to which Forster's early novels in particular drew upon and thus criticized the novels of his contemporaries.

CHAPTER 2: *SENSE AND SENSIBILITY*

1. Howard S. Babb, *Jane Austen's Novels: The Fabric of Dialogue* (1962; rpt Hamden, Conn., 1967) p. 51.
2. Norman Page, *The Language of Jane Austen* (Oxford, 1972) p. 95.
3. Marvin Mudrick, *Irony as Defense and Discovery*, p. 91.
4. Ibid.
5. Andrew Wright, *Jane Austen's Novels*, p. 89.
6. Surprisingly, this view of *Sense and Sensibility* has been long delayed, although three studies published in 1973 arrived at it independently: Tave, *Some Words of Jane Austen;* Nardin, *Elegant Decorums*, and F. B. Pinion, *A Jane Austen Companion*.
7. A. Walton Litz, *Artistic Development*, p. 76.

CHAPTER 3: *PRIDE AND PREJUDICE* AND ITS PREDECESSORS

1. Mary Lascelles, *Jane Austen and her Art*, p. 42.
2. 'Pride and Prejudice and *Cecilia*', appendix, *PP*, p. 408.
3. *Diary and Letters*, II, p. 72.
4. Q. D. Leavis, 'A Critical Theory of Jane Austen's Writings (I)', *Scrutiny*, 10 (1941);

rpt in F. R. Leavis (ed.) *A Selection from Scrutiny* (Cambridge, 1968), II, pp. 11, 12, and 13.

5. *Diary and Letters*, II, p. 154.
6. Fanny Burney, *Cecilia, or Memoirs of an Heiress* (London, 1782) VI, iii; III, 240–1. As no standard edition exists, this frist edition will be cited throughout. References will be given in the text, and will include book and chapter numbers, followed by the volume and page number of the first edition.
7. *Rambler* No. 97 (19 February 1751); *Works*, IV, 156.
8. J. M. S. Tompkins, *Popular Novel in England*, p. 103.
9. *Diary and Letters*, II, 71.
10. Ibid., p. 154.
11. Ibid., pp. 72–3.
12. J. E. Austen-Leigh, *Memoir of Jane Austen*, R. W. Chapman (ed.) (1926; rpt Oxford, 1967) p. 89.
13. *Sir Charles Grandison*, ed. and intro. Jocelyn Harris (London, 1972), I, xvii; I, 84. All references are to this edition unless otherwise noted, and are included in the text, in the form of the volume and letter numbers in editions published in Richardson's lifetime, followed by the volume and page number of the edition cited.
14. E. A. Baker, *The History of the English Novel* (1936; rpt. New York, 1966) IV, p. 74.
15. Alan D. McKillop, *Samuel Richardson: Printer and Novelist* (Chapel Hill, NC, 1936) p. 213.
16. *A Series of Letters between Mrs Elizabeth Carter and Miss Catherine Talbot, from the Year 1741 to 1770*, Montagu Pennington (ed.), 2nd ed. (London, 1809) II, 157–8. (Cited hereafter as *Carter Letters*.)
17. The temptation to draw a parallel here to Elizabeth Bennet's teaching Darcy to be laughed at is great, but should be resisted. Charlotte's laughter at Lord G is very different from Elizabeth's at Darcy; Charlotte's *can* be taken for contempt.

CHAPTER 4: *PRIDE AND PREJUDICE*

1. A few examples suffice. The novel is said to reconcile, variously, the opposing claims of 'wit and drama'; 'local complexity' and 'general clarity of design'; 'social restraint and the individual will'; 'the two extremes of "art" and "nature"'; 'civilized convention and economic primitivism'; 'morality' and 'style' (Reuben Brower, 'Light and Bright and Sparkling: Irony and Fiction in *Pride and Prejudice*, *'The Fields of Light: An Experiment in Critical Reading* [London, 1951] rpt in *Critical Essays*, p. 63; Litz, p. 106; ibid., p. 105; Samuel Kliger, 'Jane Austen's *Pride and Prejudice* in the Eighteenth-Century Mode,' *UTQ*, 16 [1947], rpt in E. Rubenstein (ed.) *Twentieth Century Interpretations of Pride and Prejudice* [Englewood Cliffs, NJ, 1969] p. 54; Dorothy Van Ghent, *The English Novel: Form and Function* [1953; rpt New York 1961] p. 105; Trilling, *'Mansfield Park*,' rpt in *Critical Essays*, p. 134). The apparent differences between these sets of terms begin to disappear when they are compared to the more generalized antithetic formulae with which critics define Austen's concerns throughout her work, for these terms correspond to or else refine such familiar balanced oppositions as head and heart, reason and feeling, judgment and fancy, society and the individual, culture and personality.

2. R. MacKinnon, cited by Chapman in 'Chronology of *Pride and Prejudice*', appendix, *PP*, pp. 400–8.

3. Mary Lascelles, *Jane Austen and her Art*, p. 163.

4. E. M. Forster makes nearly the same observation when he declares that *all* Austen's characters, even apparently 'flat' ones, 'are ready for an extended life,' in answer to his own acute question, 'Why do the characters in Jane Austen give us a slightly new pleasure each time they come in, as opposed to the merely repetitive pleasure that is caused by a character in Dickens? Why do they combine so well in a conversation, and draw one another out without seeming to do so, and never perform?' (*Aspects of the Novel* [1927; rpt New York, 1963] p. 75).

5. M. H. Abrams, *A Glossary of Literary Terms* (New York, 1957) p. 13.

6. Jane Nardin, *Elegant Decorums*, pp. 22 and 23.

7. Fanny Burney, *Memoirs of Doctor Burney* (London, 1832) II, 156.

8. Much evidence exists to show that Richardson's audience considered absolute accuracy essential in representing social conventions, and any failure in accuracy ludicrous. Elizabeth Carter, for example, congratulates her friend Catherine Talbot on having apparently made the language of *Grandison* more correct than that of *Clarissa* (*Carter Letters*, II, p. 142), but regrets that Richardson has included 'the grievous old-fashioned word *kinswoman*' (II, p. 158).

9. Samuel Richardson, 'Appendix', *Grandison*, III, p. 469.

10. S.v. 'Miss Byron', in the last volume of later contemporary editions.

11. Quoted by McKillop, *Samuel Richardson*, p. 159.

12. Alastair Duckworth, *The Improvement of the Estate* (Baltimore, 1971) p. 140.

13. Lascelles writes of this distinction that 'incongruity may be so presented to the reason as to satisfy in itself, so presented to the emotions (through sympathy) as to stir a desire which can be satisfied only by resolution of its discord' (*Jane Austen and her Art*, p. 141). The former sort of incongruity I have called comic, the latter sort emotional.

14. Whether or not Darcy's manners are polite is a central question for critics as well as for the characters in the novel. I believe that Austen intends that Darcy's manners in the first part of the novel should bear three interpretations. First, Elizabeth's: his manners are proud, unpleasant and rude. Second, an interpretation available to a candid reader even on the first reading: his manners are correct and forbearing but haughty, particularly to those he considers beneath him. Third, Darcy's own accurate estimation of them, reached at the end: his manners, however polite and correct on the surface, have lacked genuine politeness, that is, real consideration for others' feelings. Ideally, good manners prescribe and express sensitive, considerate behaviour, but Darcy's early manners are divorced from good feeling. As a result, he can be guilty of an 'unpardonable' breach of manners when he proposes to Elizabeth (367).

15. Chapman's notes to his edition of *Pride and Prejudice* suggest Boswell's *Life of Johnson* (25 April 1778) as a source for this distinction: 'All censure of a man's self is oblique praise' (*PP*, p. 392).

16. W. J. Harvey, 'The Plot of Emma', rpt in *Casebook*, p. 241.

17. Norman Page, *Language of Jane Austen*, p. 26. For alternative analyses of the dialogue in *Pride and Prejudice*, see especially Babb, pp. 113–44, and Brower, 'Light and Bright', pp. 62–75.

18. Austen's manuscript, Two Chapters of Persuasion (British Library Egerton MS. 3038), contains the first draft of Volume II, Chapter XI, which became, with a few alterations, the last chapter in the final version of the novel. This chapter is the only one in all Austen's novels for which we possess both a rough draft and the final

version. Erasures in fol. 14 of the manuscript show Austen making three attempts to end the novel on July 16, 1816, by asserting that Mrs Smith finds Captain Wentworth perfect. Austen writes successively that his aid in recovering Mrs Smith's property 'convinced her of his being much nearer Perfection than her intercourse with the World had'; 'And having done so much for her, scarcely could his wife even think him nearer perfection'; 'and having received such a benefit from him, Mrs Smith's estimate of his Perfection could be surpassed only by that Wife's'. This ending was crossed out and a new ending, substantially like the last paragraph in the final version, was added July 18. No assertion of perfection is to be found in the last pages of *Persuasion*, whereas *Emma* ends with a declaration of 'the perfect happiness of the union' (484) and *Mansfield Park* with Fanny Price living at the parsonage and finding it 'as dear to her heart, and as thoroughly perfect in her eyes, as every thing else, within the view and patronage of Mansfield Park, had long been' (473). That Austen wished to strike this note in the last sentence of *Persuasion* and decided against it fully accords with one's sense of the novel's differences from its two great predecessors.

CONCLUSION: THE LATER NOVELS

1. Q. D. Leavis, *Fiction and the Reading Public* (London, 1932) p. 256.
2. Quoted by J. E. Austen-Leigh, *Memoir*, p. 157.
3. Unsigned review of *Emma*, *Quarterly Review* 14 (1816); rpt in *Critical Heritage*, p. 68.
4. D. F. Tovey, *Essays in Musical Analysis*, 1 (1935; rpt London, 1968) pp. 61 and 62.
5. B. C. Southam, *Literary Manuscripts*, p. 121.

Index

Names of characters appear in quotation marks – for example, 'Bennet, Elizabeth'.